Offline Humans

Offline Humans

HOW TO STOP SCROLLING AND RECONNECT WITH THE REAL WORLD

NATALIE ALZATE

Publisher Mike Sanders
Executive Editor Alexander Rigby
Art & Design Director William Thomas
Editorial Director Ann Barton
Designer Lindsay Dobbs
Illustrator Samantha Silverman
Editorial Assistant Resham Anand
Development Editor Devon Fredericksen
Copy Editor Tiffany Taing
Proofreaders Jaye Debber, Michael Trudeau
Indexer Michael Goldstein

First American Edition, 2025
Published in the United States by DK Publishing
1745 Broadway, 20th Floor, New York, NY 10019

The authorized representative in the EEA is Dorling Kindersley Verlag GmbH. Arnulfstr. 124, 80636 Munich, Germany

25 26 27 28 29 10 9 8 7 6 5 4 3 2 1
001-342731-OCT2025

A catalog record for this book is available from the Library of Congress.
ISBN 978-0-5938-4700-8

Printed and bound in China

www.dk.com

This book was made with Forest Stewardship Council™ certified paper – one small step in DK's commitment to a sustainable future.
Learn more at
www.dk.com/uk/information/sustainability

**To my YouTube community,
my Outties—where it all started.
Thank you for growing with me,
both online and offline.**

Contents

Introduction

How I Became the "Offline Advocate Girlie"

Ten years ago, I started my journey as a content creator, sharing bits of my life with the online world. What started as a creative outlet turned into a full-time career—a whirlwind of creativity, connection, and if I'm being honest, exhaustion. I loved building an online community, but there was a cost. I was always "on." Suddenly it felt like every moment needed to be captured, edited, and curated for the highlight reel of my online life.

I started noticing how much time I was losing—scrolling, connecting, and chasing my next piece of content. It wasn't just my focus, though; it was my energy, clarity, and joy. I felt more excited to post about an event than to actually live it. I was overstimulated, drained, and constantly attached to my devices. Maybe you've felt it, too: the pull to stay connected even as it leaves you feeling more drained. That's when I knew something had to change.

The Digital Detox That Changed Everything

It all started with a simple experiment: One day a week, I'd go completely offline. No emails, no social media, no notifications. Just me, my thoughts, and the world around me. At first, it felt really strange—I was missing out, right? But, slowly, I started noticing the little things: the sounds of birds I'd never really heard before, the calm of reading a book without interruptions, and even my beautiful golden retriever and how he'd sadly been aging. Each detox day brought clarity and a sense of ease I hadn't felt in years. I started breathing deeper, sleeping better, and feeling more present. It was like I'd been holding my breath without realizing it, and finally I was exhaling. One day a week turned into a ritual, and that ritual became the foundation for *Offline Humans*.

Why I Wrote This Book

Offline Humans was born from my journey to reclaim my life offline. It's not about abandoning technology or demonizing social media; it's about creating space for the things that matter most—connection, presence, and joy. I've built a community of like-minded individuals who've joined me in embracing offline rituals, and this book is a way to bring that way of life to you.

Here, you'll find a mix of personal stories, practical tools, and challenges designed to help you step away from the digital noise and reconnect with yourself and the world around you. This isn't a one-size-fits-all approach; it's a guide to help you create your own rhythm and rituals, one small habit at a time.

What You'll Find in This Book

This book is organized into five parts, each designed to guide you toward a more intentional online life. Each part focuses on a specific time frame, so you can start small with your offline habits and continuously increase the amount of time you spend unplugged from the web.

Part One: Hourly–Incorporate hacks for living your life offline hour by hour.

Part Two: Daily–Turn everyday routines into soulful rituals that bring clarity and calm and that ground your days in intention and meaning.

Part Three: Weekly–Design your weekly dream days to sprinkle joy into your routine–whether with a solo recharge, creative flow, or social connection–by making intentional time for what energizes and fulfills you.

Part Four: Monthly–Embrace the rhythm of the seasons by slowing down, resetting, and finding joy in monthly hobbies that match the time of year.

Part Five: Yearly–Craft a year of mindful hobbies and seasonal moments that keep you inspired, present, and joyful all year long.

How This Book Works

This book is your go-to guide for inspiration, resets, and reminders to reconnect with yourself. Think of it as a tool to carry with you, offering a gentle nudge to unplug and live fully present. Whether you're drawn to a specific season, prompt, or activity, there's no right or wrong place to start.

This book isn't meant to be read in a specific order. Flip through and see what calls to you. Start wherever you feel drawn, and let this book be your companion on your journey to creating intentional, meaningful moments. The goal is simple: to help you pause, reflect, and embrace the beauty of living in the present.

Journal Workouts

You'll notice little Journal Workouts sprinkled throughout this book–they're like mini pit stops for your brain. Think of them as a quick stretch for your thoughts, giving you a chance to hit pause and check in with yourself. Here's how it works: Set a timer for 3 to 5 minutes, grab your journal, and dive into the prompt. It's not about perfection or writing a masterpiece–it's just a moment to clear the mental clutter and maybe uncover a nugget of wisdom. Trust me, these tiny time-outs can work wonders for keeping your mind refreshed and your thoughts flowing.

The Offline Movement

We're not just turning off our devices; we're starting a movement toward a more mindful, connected life. You don't have to do it alone. If that resonates with you, join us @OfflineHumans and let's rediscover the joy of real-life moments, together.

Part One

Hourly

Hourly Hacks for Living Life Offline

In a world that moves at lightning speed, this section is about slowing down—hour by hour. Instead of letting technology dictate your day, you'll learn to weave in micro pauses that create breathing room in your routine. Whether it's intentional screen breaks, quick movement resets, or tech-free rituals, these hourly shifts will help you reclaim your time and attention, one hour at a time.

1.

Disconnecting from Digital Life

Ready to slow down and savor the sweetness of doing nothing? In this chapter, we'll explore how to embrace the Italian concept of dolce far niente and find joy in simply being. We'll look at hourly practical steps on how to incorporate unhurried moments into your daily life and how to unplug from the internet's constant demands.

Let's take a close look and discover how to live life at 0.5 speed, finding joy and fulfillment in the present moment.

Taking Back Control of Our Technological Lives: The Hannah Montana Dilemma

We are all living in a Hannah Montana online epidemic. Remember Hannah Montana, the pop star who lived a double life as a regular high school student by day and a famous singer by night, keeping her true identity a secret? (Please tell me you know who Hannah Montana is.)

Just like Hannah, many of us are living double lives—one online and one offline. Online, we carefully curate our identities, projecting polished versions of ourselves for others to see, while offline, we're grappling with the messiness of real life. This divide between who we are and who we pretend to be can leave us feeling fragmented and disconnected from our true selves. I like to compare it to an exhausting performance, constantly switching between the highlight reel we share with the world and the more mundane or challenging realities we face offline. This duality can take a toll on our mental health and leave us feeling anxious, overextended, and struggling to keep up. When was the last time you connected deeply with yourself? If you've been feeling like you're not living in real time, you're truly not alone.

There's no doubt social media hooks our minds. It's the constant adrenaline of digital pings that stimulates us, not to mention the fear of missing out (a.k.a. "FOMO") that gives us a feeling of anxiety. It's like trying to keep up with both of Hannah's worlds at once, and it's exhausting. But here's the thing: Even Hannah Montana couldn't keep her two lives separate forever. Spoiler: Eventually she had to reveal her true self to her friends. Similarly, we need to reconcile our online and offline selves. When we don't, we risk solitude deprivation—a state where we spend almost no time alone with our thoughts, missing out on the ability to clarify problems and regulate emotions.

But here's the good news: **YOU CAN TAKE BACK CONTROL.**

Some Fun Facts

Touching phones: We touch our phones 2,617 times per day on average. (Think about it—that's more than a thousand times before lunch!)

Screen-time statistics: The average American spends around 7 hours a day glued to screens, and 3 hours and 15 minutes of that is on our phones. Between endless scrolling and Netflix binges, it's like we're stuck in our own episode of *Black Mirror*, minus the plot twist.

Even Steve Jobs had tech boundaries: Did you know that Steve Jobs didn't let his own kids use iPads? In a 2011 interview with the *New York Times*, Jobs revealed he banned his kids from using the newly released iPad, saying, "We don't allow the iPad in the home. We think it's too distracting for them." Even the tech genius himself believed in setting limits.

Mental overload: Constant switching overloads our brains and actually cripples our state of flow, which impairs our mental clarity and focus.

On average, Americans spend 3 hours and 15 minutes per day on their phones, but my screen time was a whopping 6 hours and 40 minutes a day! When I asked my online community about theirs, 6 hours seemed like nothing. The average was over 8 hours!

In a world dominated by screens and constant connectivity, taking control of our technological lives is more crucial than ever. The impact of technology on our daily routines, mental health, and relationships can be both beneficial and detrimental. Let's confront more facts about our tech-driven lives and explore the isolation that often comes with digital overload from our constant connection to screens.

Technology Use

PROS	CONS
CONNECTIVITY: Technology allows us to stay connected with loved ones, access information instantly, and communicate across the globe.	**ISOLATION:** Despite being more connected digitally, many people feel more isolated than ever.
CONVENIENCE: From online shopping to remote work, technology has made many aspects of our lives more convenient.	**MENTAL OVERLOAD:** Being online can ramp up anxiety and exhaustion from all the stimuli.
ACCESS TO RESOURCES: Educational tools, mental health resources, and creative outlets are more accessible than ever.	**DISTRACTION:** The constant notifications and the need to stay updated can lead to decreased productivity and attention spans.

The Pretty Perks of Disconnecting

Check off what you'd like to manifest in your offline journey.

- ◯ **Rediscover yourself, inside and out:** When you step away from the digital noise, you give yourself the chance to reconnect with your own thoughts and emotions.
- ◯ **Enhance intuition:** Disconnecting isn't just about slowing down; it's about finally relaxing. It's like turning up the volume on your inner voice. (Julia Cameron in *The Artist's Way* says that taking it easy helps us tune in to our emotions and intuition. So, give yourself permission to relax and listen to that inner wisdom!)
- ◯ **Increase internal dialogue:** Offline days promote a stronger connection to your internal dialogue, emotions, and intuition. It's like having a heart-to-heart with yourself.
- ◯ **Live in real time:** Living a slower-paced life is not just refreshing; it also allows you to savor each moment.
- ◯ **Rediscover old dreams:** Disconnecting can make forgotten dreams and aspirations resurface, much like reconnecting with old friends at a reunion. It's a beautiful throwback to a version of yourself.
- ◯ **Boost emotional GPS:** Unplugging acts as an update to your emotional GPS, helping you navigate life. Better clarity = better direction.
- ◯ **Set boundaries:** Recognizing that each piece of technology carries its own agenda will help you begin to be more critical of the impact and control it has on your life.

The Sweetness of Doing Nothing: Dolce Far Niente

The internet teaches us to live in constant motion—always productive, always connected. But there's a profound beauty in living an unhurried life. This concept is beautifully captured by the Italian phrase "dolce far niente," which means "the sweetness of doing nothing." It's an Italian way of living that embraces leisure and relaxation. Imagine an Italian summer: people casually basking in the sun on an early Monday afternoon, savoring the moment without rushing. They chat with friends over coffee, taking time to enjoy each other's company. This unhurried lifestyle contrasts sharply with the fast-paced, always-online mentality the internet often promotes. It's about finding joy in simply being rather than always doing.

Live an Unhurried Life

What would it feel like to live life on 0.5 speed? Take a look at the way you're currently doing life. Chances are you listen to a podcast on the way to work, double down on tasks by stacking one on another, speed through conversations, and hurry through things like meals and sleep. We're bombarded with messages to be constantly productive, to hustle, and to never stop. But there's immense value in slowing down, in savoring the moment, and in simply being. Why does this matter? There is so much fascination over fast living versus the magic of slow living—but at what cost? Slowing down isn't just a luxury; it's how we reclaim our humanity in a world that glorifies hustle.

Find "Sweet Nothings" to Enhance Your Everyday

In a world where every moment seems documented or planned, we've lost touch with the joy of simply being. Life's sweetest moments often come when we aren't actively seeking them, when we embrace spontaneity, savor small joys, and make time for reflection. These "sweet nothings" breathe life into our routines and help us truly live in the present.

As we begin to explore the magic of these sweet nothings, remember that reconnecting with the world around you doesn't require a complete life overhaul. By making space for the unplanned, savoring small moments, and stepping away from our screens, we open ourselves to the richness of offline life.

In the next chapter, we'll break this down into actionable steps to help you carve out these moments of spontaneity, reflection, and joy in your daily life, hourly. You'll find practical ways to weave these moments of mindfulness into your routine, making sweet nothings a regular part of your life.

Embrace Spontaneity

The internet tells us we need to have every moment meticulously planned and documented, but real life offers the joy of spontaneous discovery. Life isn't just about planning. Sometimes, the best moments happen when you least expect them, when you let go of the plan and just go with the flow, like when you let yourself wander without a destination, get lost in your city, or take a different route home. Small acts of spontaneity can lead to unforgettable discoveries and less daily monotony. Here's how you can find those sweet nothings in your everyday life and truly embrace the dolce far niente lifestyle.

Hourly Challenges

All of the following challenges embody the spirit of embracing spontaneity by encouraging you to go offline and shake up your routine. Think of these challenges as little sparks to ignite something new in your day. Here's a fun twist: Close your eyes, point to one mini challenge, and let it be your next small shift. Sometimes, the most refreshing moments come when you least expect it.

SPONTANEOUS OFFLINE PAUSE: Set your phone to airplane mode for an hour and see where your thoughts take you. Give yourself permission to daydream, doodle, or pick up an old hobby. Who knows? You might rediscover a long-lost passion or stumble upon your next big idea.

REVERSE A HABIT: Catch yourself in an automatic routine and flip the script. If you always reach for your phone during breaks, try grabbing a book instead. Sit in a different spot, take a new route home, or switch up your usual coffee order. Small changes bring fresh energy to your day.

SENSORY RESET: Take a quick break to fully immerse yourself in one of your senses. Smell a candle, savor the taste of your favorite drink, or listen closely to the sounds around you. This mini reset anchors you in the present moment and lets you experience life more vividly.

"NO PLAN" PAUSE: For 5 minutes, do absolutely nothing–no scrolling, no planning, no multitasking. Just sit and be. It might feel strange at first, but let your thoughts flow freely. Inspiration and clarity often emerge from moments of stillness.

Savor the Small Moments

Enjoy the little things in life, but don't go through the motions . . . immerse yourself in them. From a quiet cup of coffee or a walk in the park to a conversation with a friend, take a second to fully experience the moment. Remember that savoring these moments isn't about perfection but about gently reminding yourself to pause and experience life with all your senses. With time, these mindfulness practices can become the highlights of your day.

Hourly Challenges

This set of challenges invites you to slow down and savor the small, beautiful moments often overlooked in the rush of daily life. Explore the ideas below to cultivate a deeper connection with life's little joys, one moment at a time.

FRIENDSHIP COFFEE DATE: Invite a friend for coffee—or bring tea parties back! Feel the warmth of your coffee cup in your hands, notice the sunlight streaming through the trees, and be present in your friend's company by silencing your phone. These sweet nothings add richness to your life, but they come alive when you let yourself slow down and truly savor them.

TOUCHPOINT CONNECTION: Pause for a moment and place your hand on your chest. Notice your heartbeat or the steady rhythm of your breath. This is a simple way to reconnect with yourself and ground your thoughts.

MEMORY LANE: Grab a photo or an object that holds a special memory. Let yourself sink into that moment—what you felt, whom you were with, and why it mattered.

SILENT LISTENING: Close your eyes and tune in to the sounds around you. Maybe you hear birds outside, the hum of your fridge, or even your own breathing. Let yourself simply listen without judgment.

Digital Minimalism Philosophy

Digital minimalism is a philosophy that encourages intentional use of technology by focusing only on what adds significant value to your life. The core idea is to reduce digital clutter and distractions, allowing you to live a more focused, fulfilling, and mindful life. By adopting digital minimalism, you can reclaim your time and attention, which are often fragmented by constant digital interruptions. While we go into greater detail about how to set boundaries with technology in the next chapter, below are some simple and easy ways to incorporate digital minimalism into your life.

Batch Processing Digital Tasks

Schedule specific times of the day to check and respond to emails, social media, and messages, instead of constantly checking throughout the day.

- ★ **Purpose:** Reduces the habit of frequent checking and interruptions, helping you to focus better on tasks at hand.
- ★ **How to implement:** Allocate two or three 30-minute slots during the day for handling digital tasks. Stick to these times strictly.

Simplifying Your Digital Life

Unsubscribe from unnecessary email lists, declutter your apps, and limit your social-media accounts to only the most essential.

- ★ **Purpose:** Reduces digital clutter and minimizes distractions, making it easier to focus on what truly matters.
- ★ **How to implement:** Regularly review your digital subscriptions and apps, removing anything that doesn't add value to your life.

Intentional Social-Media Use

Set specific goals for your social-media use, such as connecting with friends, learning new things, or promoting your work, and stick to these goals.

★ **Purpose:** Ensures that your time spent on social media is purposeful and enriching, rather than a mindless scroll.

★ **How to implement:** Before logging into social media, remind yourself of your goals and set a timer to limit your use.

Analog Alternatives

Replace digital tools with analog ones wherever possible, such as using a paper planner instead of a digital calendar or reading physical books instead of ebooks.

★ **Purpose:** Encourages engagement with the physical world and reduces screen time.

★ **How to implement:** Start by identifying areas where you can switch to analog tools, and gradually make the transition.

Offline Hobbies

Develop hobbies that don't involve screens, such as painting, gardening, playing a musical instrument, or cooking. (For more on offline hobbies, see page 142.)

★ **Purpose:** Provides a fulfilling way to spend your time without digital distractions.

★ **How to implement:** Dedicate time each week to explore and practice offline hobbies. Join local clubs or groups to stay motivated and engaged.

Digital Curfews

Set a specific time in the evening when all digital devices are turned off and put away.

★ **Purpose:** Helps improve sleep quality and promotes winding down at the end of the day.

★ **How to implement:** Choose a time, such as 8 p.m. or 9 p.m., and make it a household rule. Engage in calming activities, like reading or meditating, before bed.

Unplug to Revive Your Hobbies

To whoever needs to hear this: If you feel overwhelmed and overstimulated by constant notifications and social media, you're not alone. I've been there, too. Taking control of my tech use completely transformed my life. Those quiet, disconnected moments gave me the time and energy to study, read, and dive deeper into activities I genuinely enjoy. I've started cooking, gardening, language learning, taking salsa classes, and rock climbing. Journaling has also become a daily ritual, a truly sacred moment for me to pause and reflect.

There's something refreshing about experiencing a moment purely for what it is—not to capture it and share it but simply to be there. There's a difference between being there and being there to get "the shot." Nurturing your approach to this will help you avoid seeking validation from others online. And you'd be surprised how much time you get back when you stop endlessly scrolling. Suddenly, there's room for the things that truly enrich your life, and you have so much more time for what truly matters.

I won't sugarcoat it: Stepping away from screens can be tough at first. But the shift is life-changing. My mental health has improved, and I feel calmer, more focused, and genuinely happier. So, if you feel like you're drowning in digital overload, take a step back. Reclaim your time, and rediscover the joy in your hobbies and passions.

Where do you start? What should you avoid? Don't worry—in the next chapter, we'll break it all down.

Key Takeaways

THE HANNAH MONTANA DILEMMA: We live double lives—carefully curated online personas versus our offline realities—leading to disconnection, anxiety, and solitude deprivation.

TECH OVERLOAD: With an average daily screen time of over 7 hours, our constant connection to screens harms our mental health, flow states, and emotional clarity.

DOLCE FAR NIENTE: The Italian concept of "the sweetness of doing nothing" invites us to embrace slower living, savor spontaneous moments, and find joy in being present.

THE BEAUTY OF DISCONNECTING: Disconnecting from technology allows us to rediscover intuition, reconnect with ourselves, and live in real time.

PROS AND CONS OF TECHNOLOGY: While technology offers convenience and connectivity, overuse can also isolate us, overload our minds, and keep us in a perpetual state of distraction.

REDISCOVERING OFFLINE JOY: Simple practices like morning rituals, journaling, and offline adventures help us reconnect with ourselves and those around us.

Action Items

- Create morning and evening rituals. Begin your day with calming rituals (for example, a Gratitude Tea Time ritual).
- Curate your feed for growth. Search for uplifting content (like "how to stop doomscrolling" or "screenless hobbies") to train your algorithm toward positive inspiration.
- Practice mindful posting. Limit posting moments online. Live for the experience, not the 'Gram.
- Reevaluate your hobbies. List hobbies you've abandoned, and set aside time to revisit one this week.
- Plan one daily offline activity. Dedicate an hour each day to an offline hobby, like reading, baking, or going for a tech-free walk.

Notes

2

Setting Boundaries

We've all been there—we plan to take a quick peek at our phones only to find ourselves lost in a whirlwind of notifications, social-media posts, and endless scrolling. It's not just a time thief; it's an energy zapper that leaves us mentally drained and craving balance. The good news? Setting boundaries with your screen time isn't about cutting technology out of your life entirely—it's about using it intentionally, on your terms, and learning how to quiet the digital noise so you can focus on what matters. By identifying where your attention is being hijacked and implementing mindful changes, you'll feel more in control of your time and energy. In this chapter, we'll explore how to stay grounded and fully present, even when your device is calling for attention. Let's gear up for a digital reset and discover practical exercises to help you unplug, reconnect, and take control.

Stolen Focus

To reclaim our attention, we need to be honest about what is really stealing it. The first step to fixing a bad habit is acknowledging it. Think of tiny changes like planting seeds—at first, they might not seem like much, but with patience and care, they can grow into something amazing over time.

So today, we're going to take a look at where you stand. The more honest you are in this assessment, the better equipped you will be to break these ties. Lastly, we'll compile a list of small habits and cues that add to negative behaviors.

Let's play a little game—you've probably seen it floating around online. It's called Put a Finger Down. Starting with all ten of your fingers out, put a finger down if you:

- ★ Check your phone within 5 minutes of waking up.
- ★ Snap a picture of your food before you eat.
- ★ Scroll through social media while eating.
- ★ Use your phone in the bathroom.
- ★ Automatically reach for your phone during any free moment.
- ★ Check social media during conversations with friends or family.
- ★ Feel the need to post about every event or activity you attend.
- ★ Lose track of time while scrolling through your feed.
- ★ Sleep with your phone next to your bed.
- ★ Use your phone as a way to avoid awkward situations.

How many fingers do you have left?
Let's see how you rank:

8 to 10 fingers left: Digital Zen Master: You've got great control over your tech habits! Keep being the calm in the digital storm.

4 to 7 fingers left: Guilty Scroller: You're doing okay, but those thumbs have a mind of their own sometimes. Let's tighten up those boundaries!

0 to 3 fingers left: Phone Zombie: Technology has taken over! Time to reclaim your brain and break free from the screen's grip.

Whether you're a Digital Zen Master who checked off only 2 items or a Phone Zombie who perhaps checked off 7 out of 10, it's important to acknowledge where you stand and take steps toward improvement.

Negative Impacts of Stolen Focus

Let's list the ways that not setting boundaries with social media may be impacting your life. If you can't think of any, check off the ones below that apply to you, and then follow the subsequent guide to start addressing them.

- ◯ Experiencing mental fatigue from overstimulation
- ◯ Struggling to enjoy real-life moments because of the urge to document everything
- ◯ Feeling isolated despite being digitally connected
- ◯ Not prioritizing time for hobbies
- ◯ Feeling unsatisfied with life's accomplishments
- ◯ Losing control of health (e.g., neglecting to schedule breaks for exercise)
- ◯ Mismanaging sleep quality and length (you know you could do better!)
- ◯ Not seeing or connecting with friends
- ◯ Reflecting at the end of the year and realizing your goals haven't been met
- ◯ Constantly feeling tired or experiencing FOMO for people's accomplishments online
- ◯ Feeling anxious without constant connectivity
- ◯ Focusing poorly on tasks due to digital distractions

Digital Burnout? Reset and Recharge with These Simple Steps

Mental fatigue
Set screen-time limits and take regular breaks.

Not prioritizing hobbies
Block time daily for offline activities.

Poor sleep quality
Set a no-screen policy an hour before bed.

Anxious without connectivity
Try mindfulness exercises to ease digital anxiety.

Struggling with real-life moments
Limit phone use and savor the moment.

Comparing your accomplishments to others'
Reflect weekly and celebrate the small wins.

Goals not met by year's end
Set and review weekly milestones.

Distracted by devices
Use app blockers or focus techniques like the Pomodoro method.

Feeling isolated
Plan in-person meetups with those you love.

Losing control of health
Schedule movement breaks throughout the day.

FOMO or constant tiredness
Practice gratitude journaling regularly.

Boundaries with Screen Time

Establishing boundaries with technology is a vital self-care practice, but finding a healthy balance with screen time can feel like walking a tightrope—one wrong step, and suddenly hours have disappeared into the digital abyss. We know we need boundaries to help protect our mental and emotional well-being and to allow ourselves to recharge and find balance in our daily lives. To do so, we need to identify the exact challenges we face with our devices. Is it boredom? The constant stream of notifications? Or maybe it's that nagging fear of missing out on what's happening online. Whatever it is, acknowledging the hurdles is the first step toward reclaiming your time and attention.

Journal Workout

Use the following prompts to dig into your relationship with screen time and uncover where those boundaries might need a little reinforcement.

What impact does checking your phone first thing in the morning have on the rest of your day?

After a long session on your phone, how are you feeling? Are you refreshed and inspired, or is your brain mushy from mindless scrolling? If it's the latter, how can you mix it up next time?

How do you feel when you're standing in line without your phone? What thoughts or emotions arise in that moment?

When you're in a social situation, how do you use your phone? What role does it play in your interactions with others?

When you're procrastinating with your phone, what emotions or tasks are you avoiding? How might you address them differently?

Which parts of your day tend to be hijacked by your screen? Are you reaching for your phone at meals, when hanging with friends, or while trying to unwind? What boundaries could help you stay more present?

What would a day without your phone look like? How would it challenge you, and what opportunities might it offer?

How can you give your phone a break without feeling like you're missing out? Can you create mini phone-free zones, like at the dinner table or during your morning routine? What would that look like?

What hobbies have been gathering dust while your phone gets all the attention? Remember when you used to enjoy reading, cooking, or maybe playing guitar? How can you bring some of that fun back into your day?

Remember, you're not alone. In our hyperconnected world, it's easy to feel overwhelmed and consumed by our screens. Many of us struggle with finding a healthy balance between our digital lives and real-world experiences. If you've ever felt like your phone is taking over, you're not the only one. Below are some common crutches you might be using. Check off the ones that resonate with you.

Common Crutches Checklist

- ◯ I often find myself mindlessly scrolling through my phone when I'm bored or need an escape.
- ◯ My mornings feel odd without digital distractions to ease me into the day.
- ◯ I feel pressured to share my life on social media before processing my experiences.
- ◯ I realize I miss out on real-life moments because I'm trying to capture them on my phone.
- ◯ I spend almost no time alone with my own thoughts.
- ◯ I frequently compare my life to other people's curated lives on social media, which affects my self-esteem.
- ◯ I feel anxious or stressed when I can't check my phone.
- ◯ I often procrastinate on important tasks because I'm distracted by social media.
- ◯ I feel a constant need to stay up to date with the latest posts and news on social media.
- ◯ I use my phone as a way to avoid social interactions or uncomfortable situations.
- ◯ I have trouble sleeping because I use my phone late into the night.
- ◯ I find it difficult to focus on tasks without checking my phone frequently.
- ◯ I feel guilty or regretful after spending too much time on social media.
- ◯ I struggle to enjoy activities without documenting or sharing them on social media.
- ◯ I experience FOMO when I see posts about events or activities I didn't attend.

Digital-Detox Exercises

The first step to creating tech boundaries is realizing how much dependence we have on our phones. Are we taking it into the bathroom with us? Are we getting online first thing in the morning? If you've been meaning to find a way not to be so dependent on your phone or mindlessly scroll when you're bored, here are some interactive examples of hourly exercises to help you disconnect.

Morning Routine Reset

Instead of reaching for your phone, start your day with a morning ritual that encourages mindfulness, such as stretching, journaling, or having breakfast. For instance, my Gratitude Tea Time ritual involves making a cup of tea, holding the warm mug, and reflecting on three things I'm grateful for. Dedicate the first 30 minutes to something mindful and fulfilling.

One tip that has made a big difference for me is sticking to a "no social media" rule before 10 a.m. and after 10 p.m. This simple boundary helps me start the day with clarity and end it with a sense of calm. During these times, I focus on building the habits that align with the life I want to lead, like waking up earlier, journaling, or planning for the day ahead. If you're curious about how I stay consistent, I use the "Best Me Routine" section of the *My Best Me Journal* to track my progress. There's something so motivating about checking off each habit; it's a small win that makes a big impact on how productive and accomplished I feel.

Journal Workout

Take 3 to 5 minutes to design your ideal morning routine without screens. What activities would help you start your day feeling refreshed and focused? Write down three habits you'd like to include in your morning—like stretching, journaling, or enjoying a slow breakfast. *Bonus: Reflect on how these habits could set a positive tone for your entire day.*

The Phone-Free Power Hour

Take control of your time with a dedicated 1-hour break from your phone each day. Instead of letting notifications dictate your focus, you choose when to unplug. Whether it's during meals, deep work, or winding down before bed, this structured reset helps clear mental clutter and refocus your energy.

1. Pick your hour. Identify a time when you tend to mindlessly scroll—maybe during lunch, right before bed, or while waiting in line. Choose an hour today to switch your phone to "Do Not Disturb" mode.

2. Turn off notifications. Reclaim your attention by silencing distractions.

3. Replace with an offline activity. Read a book, go for a walk, journal, or have an uninterrupted conversation.

4. Repeat daily. This small habit adds up, training your brain to be more mindful with screen use.

Bonus: If an hour feels too long at first, start with 30 minutes and build up over time.

Designated Tech-Free Zones

Establish areas of your home (like the bedroom or dining table) where phones and digital devices are not allowed, encouraging more intentional and mindful living.

Practicing Mindfulness

No more multitasking: Next time you're waiting in a line or caught in traffic, take it as an opportunity. Instead of scrolling through your phone, let your mind wander, enjoy the quiet, and just think. You can also try incorporating simple mindfulness techniques, such as the following.

- ★ **Body scan:** Mentally check in with your body from head to toe. Notice any areas of tension or discomfort, and consciously release those areas as you go.
- ★ **Five senses check-in:** Bring your attention to each of your five senses, one at a time. What can you see, hear, feel, smell, and taste? This exercise can ground you in the present moment and heighten your awareness of the world around you.
- ★ **Mantra repetition:** Choose a calming word or phrase (like "peace" or "calm"), and repeat it silently to yourself, aligning it with your breathing to center your thoughts.
- ★ **Visualizing calm:** Picture a peaceful place in your mind—a beach, a forest, or any setting that brings you a sense of calm. (For me, it's my dog Jupiter.) Imagine yourself there, soaking in the sights, sounds, and feelings of tranquility.
- ★ **Hand meditation:** Focus your attention on your hands, noticing the temperature, texture, and sensations. You can slowly rub them together or gently press your fingertips together, paying close attention to every sensation.
- ★ **People watching:** Engage in a quiet observation of the world around you—notice the details of your surroundings, the expressions on people's faces, or even just the movement and flow of life happening around you.

Digital-Detox Hour

Pick an hour each evening to completely unplug from digital devices. What hour will this week's be?

I commit to unplugging at:

App Time Limits

On social media apps, set daily usage limits to prevent overconsumption and encourage more mindful browsing.

Saturdays have become my go-to digital-detox days, when I set all the time limits for my apps to zero. It's surprising how often you don't realize you've slipped into the habit of grabbing your phone and opening an app until you're already deep in the scroll. Regardless of the time limit you choose, having those "STOP" reminders pop up can be a game-changer, gently nudging you to step back and stay present.

Limit Notifications

Turn off nonessential notifications to reduce the number of interruptions throughout the day and reclaim mental space. Start by disabling alerts for social-media apps, news updates, and promotional emails—anything that doesn't require immediate attention. Instead, set specific times to check these apps.

Journal Workout

Take 3 to 5 minutes to reflect on which notifications tend to interrupt your day the most. Write down a list of apps or alerts that you check out of habit and ask yourself, *Do I really need to see these immediately?* Once you've identified the biggest distractions, jot down two specific time windows—one in the morning and one later in the day—when you'll check these apps. This simple boundary can help you reclaim focus and stay intentional with your time.

"Do Not Disturb" Mode

Set your phone to "Do Not Disturb" during meals, times of focus, and personal moments to minimize interruptions. During my focus work hours, I set blocks of uninterrupted time, kind of like putting up a "No Trespassing" sign for distractions. But here's the trick: To avoid ending the day with a mountain of unanswered messages that feel like a game of inbox Jenga, carve out two response windows, one in the morning and one in the evening. Think of this practice as giving your brain its much-needed spa time while still staying connected and reliable.

The goal here isn't to ghost people until you feel like answering. Being responsive, within reason, helps others trust you and see you as dependable, like that one friend who always texts back with the perfect meme. Some of the most successful people I know tackle questions right away, treating them like mini fires they'd rather put out immediately than let pile up into a wildfire of to-dos.

Embrace Old Tech

Use technology that doesn't connect to the internet. For example, listen to music on a record player or take photos with a digital camera that doesn't have internet access.

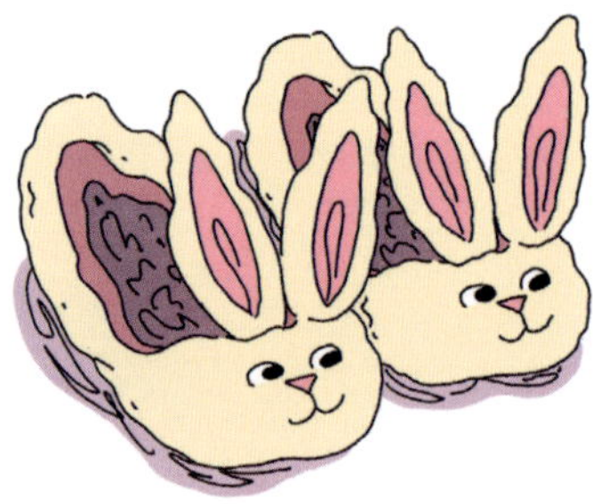

Bedtime Routine

Put your phone to sleep 1 hour before you put yourself to sleep. Yes, give it a little bed in another room and tuck it away. Establish a calming bedtime routine that doesn't involve your phone. Let's brainstorm some relaxing activities to incorporate into your evening.

- ★ **Reading:** Pick up a physical book or magazine, and enjoy some quiet reading time.
- ★ **Stretching/yoga:** Engage in gentle stretching or a short yoga session to relax your body and mind.
- ★ **Meditation:** Practice mindfulness or guided meditation to unwind and clear your mind.
- ★ **Journaling:** Reflect on your day by writing in a journal. You can jot down thoughts, feelings, or plans for the next day.
- ★ **Bathing:** Take a warm bath or shower to soothe your muscles and prepare for sleep.
- ★ **Creative activities:** Try drawing, knitting, or another quiet hobby that helps you relax.
- ★ **Gratitude practice:** Write down a few things you're grateful for, reflecting on the positives of your day.

Journal Workout

What's one small step you can take tonight to start a phone-free bedtime routine? Imagine how refreshed you'd feel after just a week of phone-free evenings. What's the first activity you'd incorporate to unwind without your phone?

____

____

____

____

____

Common Struggles with Digital Detox

Think of your phone as that overly clingy friend who's always around. You wake up, and there they are, waiting to tell you the latest gossip, to remind you about yesterday's drama, or simply to demand your attention without offering anything meaningful in return. It's not that you dislike them; it's just that sometimes you need space. Like, real space—without notifications, updates, and endless scrolling. But just like with that friend, it's hard to set boundaries, and before you know it, you've spent hours together without really meaning to.

Digital detoxing isn't about breaking up with your phone—let's face it, we're in a lifelong relationship with technology—but it's more like setting healthy boundaries with that clingy friend so you can actually enjoy your life without constant interruption. From the urge to check Instagram the moment your eyes open to the never-ending scrolling at night, we've all been there. And just like with any good friend, some space could actually make the relationship better. Here are some of the most common tech challenges and the solutions that can help you reclaim your time.

PROBLEM

You begin scrolling right after waking up.

SOLUTION

Start your day on your terms, not your phone's. Try using an actual alarm clock (yes, they still exist!), and keep your phone across the room. That way, when you wake up, you're not instantly bombarded by notifications. Instead, give yourself a few moments of peace before diving into the digital world.

PROBLEM

You find yourself mindlessly scrolling when you're bored, need an escape, or want to keep up with everyone else.

SOLUTION

Let's break the solution down based on what's pulling you toward your phone:

- ★ **Boredom:** Instead of reaching for your phone, keep a list of quick activities that genuinely interest you. I started a hobbies closet, and just opening the door brings me so much joy. It's stocked with paint-by-numbers, embroidery kits, micro mosaics, magic model clay, and glitter. Basically, it's a crafty girl's dream! Having a dedicated space filled with offline activities that spark joy is so underrated. It serves as a go-to for moments when I'm tempted to mindlessly scroll but crave something more fulfilling. You could choose anything from reading a few pages of a book to learning a new skill, or even doing a 5-minute stretch. Keep this list handy so when boredom strikes, you have something more engaging to turn to than just endless scrolling.
- ★ **Need an escape:** We all need a break sometimes, but let's face it: Mindless scrolling rarely leaves us feeling refreshed. Instead, give yourself a brain break, simply a short pause to rest and recharge your mind. Think of this break as hitting the reset button for your brain, helping you feel clearer and more focused. Want something simple and immediate? Try a 5-minute walk, or put on your favorite playlist and let the music transport you. Later in this book, you'll find outdoor activities like shadow tracing with nature, which can turn a flower you find into inspiration for a work of art.

* **Keeping up with everyone else:** FOMO is real, but instead of scrolling through other people's highlight reels, flip the script. Set aside specific times in your day to catch up intentionally. Maybe it's a 10-minute check-in, then you're done. In the meantime, focus on creating moments in your own life that make you feel fulfilled—without the pressure of keeping up. If you want to take it a step farther, create a list of people you follow who consistently inspire and uplift you. By curating your feed, you take control of the feelings that come from consuming content, making it a tool for growth and positivity rather than comparison or FOMO. However, this doesn't mean you should only follow people who share the same perspectives or viewpoints as you. It's about intentionally choosing what the internet feeds you, ensuring it adds value and balance to your life without overwhelming you.

PROBLEM

You wake up feeling stressed and overwhelmed by the day ahead, immediately jumping into a flurry of notifications, emails, and tasks, which sets a frantic tone for your morning.

SOLUTION

Slow down and create a space for a smoother start to your day. If rushing through your morning has become a habit, try waking up earlier. Start with just 15 to 30 minutes, and gradually build to a full hour before your workday. But here's the secret: Your morning begins the night before with what I call the closing shift. (For a breakdown on what the closing shift is, see page 51 in chapter 3.)

PROBLEM

Your anxiety and overwhelm are at an all-time high, and it feels like your mind is racing a mile a minute. You need space, time to think, and rest.

SOLUTION

It's time to hit the pause button. Start with deep breathing—inhale for a count of four, hold, and exhale slowly. Even small acts of self-care, like stepping outside for fresh air, journaling about what's on your mind, or indulging in a calming ritual (hello, tea break), can help you recharge. The goal is to create pockets of peace in your day so you can refocus and relax. You deserve moments of joy and relaxation—give yourself permission to take them. I'll be the first to say that this doesn't always work for everyone. Breathing exercises can be helpful, but for those of us with busy minds, sitting still and focusing on our breaths might feel more frustrating than calming—and that's okay.

Sometimes, what I really need is time with a friend to rant, gossip, or just talk things through. Why? Because venting isn't only about unloading your thoughts—it's a way of processing them out loud, finding clarity, and getting some perspective. Gossiping (in a lighthearted, nonharmful way) can be a surprising form of emotional release, reminding you that you're not alone, that others go through messy situations, too, and that it's okay to laugh about life's absurdities.

The value isn't in the venting alone, but rather in the connection, the shared understanding, and the sense of being heard. It's a reminder that you don't have to carry everything on your own. Whether you grab coffee with a friend, exchange voice notes, or call someone who "gets it," know that leaning on others can be just as grounding as any solo ritual. The key is to find what genuinely helps you feel lighter and more at peace.

PROBLEM

Social media has a sneaky way of distorting reality. Suddenly, you're scrolling through perfectly curated feeds, and boom—you're feeling like your life doesn't quite measure up to that influencer who seems to have it all figured out. Sound familiar?

SOLUTION

First off, remember that social media is a highlight reel, not the full story. Cut back on your usage if it's making you feel down, and curate your feed with accounts that lift you up. Follow people who inspire you, not just those who show off a perfect life. And whenever you feel that comparison creeping in, remind yourself that social media often presents a filtered, distorted view of reality (nobody's life is as flawless as it looks on Instagram!), then pause and ask yourself: Is this inspiring me, or is it making me feel worse?

If it's the latter, take action. Unfollow accounts that leave you feeling drained or inadequate, and replace them with ones that bring you joy, teach you something new, or make you feel empowered. Diversify your feed by following people with different perspectives, hobbies, or lifestyles—this can help you break free from the constant loop of needing to be perfect.

Journal Workout

Take 5 minutes to reflect on the following question: How do I want social media to make me feel? Write down the emotions or vibes you want to experience from your social media—like inspired, motivated, or connected. Next, make a list of five accounts that currently inspire you or align with those feelings. Then, spend five minutes reviewing the accounts you follow and reassess. Unfollow any accounts that don't match the energy or positivity you noted. This simple reset can help you create a feed that lifts you up instead of bringing you down.

PROBLEM

You feel pressure to share about a life experience before you've even processed it.

SOLUTION

Focus on enjoying moments for what they are instead of feeling the need to document everything. Give yourself permission to be present without capturing every detail.

Take it from me—I used to feel this constant pressure to share every life milestone immediately, whether it was a vacation, a special dinner, or a quiet moment at home. Now, I give myself space to process and enjoy. The photos and stories can wait. Sometimes, the most meaningful memories are the ones we keep for ourselves, without the added pressure of sharing them with the world right away.

PROBLEM

You miss real-life moments because you're so preoccupied with capturing them on your phone.

SOLUTION

Make a conscious effort to be present during significant moments. Sometimes, that means leaving your phone in the car or at home altogether. If that feels too risky or inconvenient, take your phone with you but try moving your camera and video apps to a different folder or screen. This small adjustment makes you more aware when you instinctively reach for those apps, helping you to resist the urge to capture every moment. Engage with your surroundings and the people you are with rather than your phone.

PROBLEM

Fear of missing out has you feeling like you need to be everywhere, all the time. Your schedule becomes so jam-packed with activities, social media, and events that you end up stressed, overwhelmed, and retreating into your phone for an escape.

SOLUTION

Shift your mindset to focus on the present moment. It's okay to miss out on some things—life isn't about catching every moment but about being fully present for the ones that matter. Take a step back, breathe, and let yourself enjoy where you are right now instead of constantly chasing what's next. Shift your perspective to instead embrace "JOMO"—the joy of missing out. Think about the activities you often push aside when you're caught up in app scrolling or simply feel too lazy to do. For me, it's walking into my library and picking up a great book. Or instead of posting my latest photo dump to my feed, I'll print out the photos and add them to my scrapbook journal. Seeing those moments come to life again is such a fun and creative way to relive them.

PROBLEM

You've noticed that your mind is constantly filled with noise from the outside world, leaving little to no time for your own thoughts. This makes it harder to clear your head, solve problems, or regulate your emotions.

SOLUTION

It's time to create space for yourself. Schedule regular moments of solitude—5 minutes in the morning or a walk during lunch, for instance. Use this time to reflect, let your mind wander, or jump into something calming that brings you peace and clarity. The world can wait while you take a breather.

Journal Workout

Take 5 minutes to reflect on the following question: What are some activities I've been putting off because I'm too caught up in social media or the fear of missing out? Write down three to five activities that bring you joy. Now, choose one of these activities and plan when you'll do it this week. *Bonus: Journal about how you feel after completing it, and notice how it brings a sense of calm and fulfillment.*

Posting Online vs. Checking Inside

In the age of social media, the urge to post every moment online can overshadow the joy of actually living it. Why do we feel the need to document every moment? Let's explore the aspects of living for the 'Gram and how you can flip that into living for yourself.

Social Validation

It's easy to get caught up in trying to capture the perfect shot for social media. But this often leads to missing out on the real experience.

Hourly Challenge

LIVING IN THE MOMENT: The next time you're doing something out of the ordinary—trying a new restaurant, spending time with loved ones, or even taking a quiet walk—resist the urge to capture it. No photos, no videos—just immerse yourself in the moment. See how it feels to let go of the need to document and simply experience.

Hypnotic Short-Form Videos

These quick little videos are like snacks for your brain, easy to consume, but somehow you end with a whole feast of content before you even realize it. Next thing you know, time's flown by, and you've watched way more than you planned.

Short-form videos on social media have a unique way of capturing your attention, don't they? Before you know it, minutes turn into hours as you get lost in an endless stream of content. They're designed to be addictive, pulling you in with quick, engaging snippets that are hard to resist. This constant barrage of fast-paced videos can leave you feeling mentally drained and distracted, making it difficult to focus on anything else. It's incredible how such brief content can have such a powerful hold on your attention, often leaving you feeling more scattered than before.

Hourly Challenges

CONTROL YOUR ALGORITHM: If you find yourself watching content, use the ideas below to take control of your algorithm. Start curating it to reflect the things you want to learn or explore. Think of it as reshaping your feed to support the habits, goals, or dreams you've been meaning to pursue. Search for topics that match the person you want to become, and let your feed work for you, not against you.

- ★ How to wake up earlier
- ★ Tips to stop doomscrolling
- ★ Screen-free hobbies to try
- ★ Trip ideas for ________________ [insert your dream destination]
- ★ Books that will alter your brain chemistry
- ★ Easy home-organization tips
- ★ How to plan your dream solo trip
- ★ How to build confidence in daily life
- ★ Solo date ideas to reconnect with yourself
- ★ How to start learning a new language
- ★ Tips for emotional intelligence
- ★ Local hidden gems in ____________ [insert your city]
- ★ Daily affirmations for a mindset shift

DEEP CONNECTION: Think about something you've been wanting to learn more about for years. What is it? Why haven't you gone for it? How can you dedicate 1 hour this coming week to researching and dreaming about it?

Reflect and Explore

Now that you've started setting boundaries with technology, it's time to reflect on how these changes are affecting your daily life. Journaling is a powerful way to track your progress, identify challenges, and uncover deeper insights into your relationship with technology. By taking a moment each day to answer these journal prompts, you'll create a space for self-awareness and mindful adjustment as you continue your journey toward a more intentional offline life.

Journal Workout

What's the hardest part of carving out "unplugged" time for yourself?

How can you make it feel more sustainable in your daily routine?

When you avoid using your phone in bed or in the bathroom, what do you experience instead? *Bonus: Reflect on how these habits could set a positive tone for your entire day.*

Key Takeaways

RECOGNIZING DIGITAL BURNOUT: Explore common signs of tech overuse, from mental fatigue to poor sleep, and see how they may affect your life.

RECOGNIZING SCREEN-TIME CHALLENGES: Identify the habits and moments where your screen takes over, such as mindless scrolling, FOMO, or feeling pressured to document everything. Reflect on which habits resonate and how they affect your daily life.

RECOGNIZING DIGITAL DISTRACTIONS: Identify the habits that pull you away from being present, such as scrolling on your phone first thing in the morning or mindlessly checking social media.

SETTING HEALTHY BOUNDARIES: Implement practical steps like keeping your phone away from your bed, using an actual alarm clock, and carving out phone-free times during the day.

MANAGING FOMO AND SOCIAL-MEDIA COMPARISONS: Instead of trying to be everywhere at once, focus on the moments that matter most to you. It's okay to miss out on some things in order to fully enjoy the present. Remember that social media is often a highlight reel, not reality. Follow accounts that uplift and inspire you, and take breaks when comparisons start to bring you down.

MAKING SPACE FOR SOLITUDE AND MINDFUL ESCAPES: Make room for quiet moments throughout your day, be it 5 minutes of reflection or a peaceful walk. Use this time to think, breathe, and reconnect with yourself. When you need a break, turn to activities that truly relax and refresh you—like listening to music, or spending time on a hobby—rather than turning to your phone for distraction.

STARTING YOUR DAY MINDFULLY: Begin each morning with a ritual that grounds you, like making a cup of tea, stretching, or reflecting on what you're grateful for. This sets a calm tone for your day ahead.

Action Items

- Complete the Common Crutches Checklist to identify your screen-time triggers.
- Implement a morning routine reset with 3 mindful activities.
- Commit to a daily digital-detox hour, and brainstorm 3 engaging offline activities.
- Establish a phone-free bedtime routine with relaxing alternatives.
- Go through your most-used apps and add screen-time limits on those.
- Schedule one JOMO (joy of missing out) activity into your planner this week.
- Choose a morning ritual and practice your ritual daily for 7 days.
- Schedule daily "Do Not Disturb" times for focused offline work.
- At the next event you attend, challenge yourself not to capture any of it. Either leave your phone behind or rearrange your camera apps to help you make a conscious effort to stay present.
- Conduct a social-media audit, and create a list of people you follow who uplift and inspire you.

Notes

3

Hacking Your Habits

Systems That Make Life Easier

In this chapter, we'll explore how small, consistent actions can lead to major transformations. Instead of viewing habits as overwhelming lifestyle changes, we'll break them down into micro adjustments—hourly resets that help reinforce positive behaviors throughout the day.

With recommendations like setting up cues that make good habits easier and sticking to routines that reduce screen time, this chapter will guide you in designing a system that works with your natural rhythms. You'll learn how to integrate habit stacking, environmental design, and digital minimalism to create seamless, automatic behaviors that align with your goals.

By the end, you'll have practical strategies to make habits feel effortless, allowing you to build momentum and lasting change—one small shift at a time.

Understanding Habits

Often, we underestimate the power of small, consistent actions. It's easy to think that minor adjustments won't make a significant difference, but this couldn't be farther from the truth. Just like a single drop of water can eventually carve out a canyon, tiny changes, when maintained over time, can lead to profound transformations in our lives.

Consider the act of reading just one page of a book each night. At first glance, it might seem insignificant, but over the course of a year, this habit could result in finishing several books. Think of it as planting a seed. At first, you may not see much happening. But with regular watering and care, that seed will eventually grow into a strong, healthy plant. The same goes for your daily rhythms. Instead of thinking about habits only in terms of major life overhauls, try viewing them as **hourly resets**—micro adjustments throughout the day that gradually build into powerful transformations.

The key is consistency. Sticking with these small changes, even when they don't show immediate results, is crucial. Over time, they build upon each other, creating momentum and leading to significant improvements. It's the small, hourly shifts—going away from screens, taking mindful breaks, or moving your body—that accumulate into meaningful progress. This concept is often referred to as the "compound effect."

By embracing small changes and committing to them over the long term, you set the stage for remarkable results. It's not about making drastic overnight changes; it's about the steady accumulation of positive actions that lead to lasting change. Every hour presents an opportunity to reset and realign with the habits that matter most.

Cue and Habit Initiation: Small Shifts Every Hour

A habit is initiated by a cue. When the cues that spark a habit are subtle or hidden, they are easy to ignore. To build positive habits, it's essential to make the cues for those habits more obvious and prominent in your environment.

For instance, if you want to develop the habit of drinking more water, place a water bottle on your desk where you can see it all day. This visual cue will remind you to take a sip regularly. On the other hand, if you want to reduce your screen time before bed, consider placing your phone in another room so that the cue to check it is less accessible.

The trick is to think in smaller increments—not just daily goals but hourly ones. What small shift can you make every hour to reinforce your desired habits? Instead of trying to be more active in general, set a reminder to stretch or walk every hour. If your goal is to be more mindful, use hourly cues—like a sip of tea, a breath, or a screen-free moment—to reset your focus.

By deliberately designing your environment to highlight positive cues and minimize negative ones, you can make it easier to initiate and maintain healthy habits. These hourly resets create momentum, helping habits feel like natural extensions of your routine rather than something forced. Remember, make your cues obvious, and watch how these micro adjustments lead to lasting positive changes in your life.

Set Up Hourly Cues

Think of this as setting up little breadcrumbs to lead you straight to your goals. Want to read more? Toss a book on your pillow so it's the last thing you see before bed. Trying to sneak in more steps during the day? Park your sneakers by the door so it's like they're daring you to take them for a spin. The idea is to make your habits impossible to ignore, putting your intentions on a flashing billboard just for you.

And here's the fun flip side: If you're trying to cut down on something, make it harder to access. Want to scroll less? Toss your phone in a drawer while working, and voilà—you've just made a distraction harder to reach. These tiny tweaks don't just apply daily—they can work hourly, too. If you want to improve focus, set an hourly reminder to take a deep breath or stretch. Looking to stay hydrated? Use a brightly colored water bottle as a cue to take a sip every hour. The goal is to turn good intentions into automatic actions, integrating these resets throughout the day rather than relying on sheer willpower.

Examples of Making Habits Obvious

Place a book on your bedside table to encourage nighttime reading.

Keep your workout clothes by your bed to remind you to exercise in the morning.

Put a journal and pen on your kitchen table to prompt morning writing.

Set a physical alarm clock on your nightstand instead of your phone.

Display a calendar or planner prominently to remind you of your daily schedule.

Set an hourly reminder on your smartwatch or phone to take a deep breath, hydrate, or stretch. A great way to break this up is via the Pomodoro method, where you focus on a task for 25 minutes without distractions, followed by a short 5-minute break.

Small Hourly Cues to Help Reduce Screen Time

- ★ **Weekly screen-time review:** Set a weekly reminder to review your screen time and reflect on your usage patterns. Use this time to set goals for reducing unnecessary screen time.
- ★ **Digital-detox day:** Set an alarm for an allotted "Offline Reset" day each week when you completely unplug from digital devices. You can start small by doing hourly offline resets, even if for just 10-minute intervals.
- ★ **Dedicated phone zone:** Create a designated area in your home, like a basket or drawer, to place your phone an hour before bedtime. This can help reduce late-night scrolling and improve sleep quality.
    - **CUE:** Set a low-light lamp or salt lamp near the phone zone, and switch it on when you put your phone away. The change in ambient lighting acts as a cue to shift into relaxation mode.
- ★ **Visual reminders:** Place sticky notes in frequently visited areas with reminders such as "Take a break," "Go for a walk," or "Read a book" to encourage screen-free activities.
- ★ **Charging station:** Set up a charging station outside your bedroom to charge your phone overnight. This helps prevent the temptation to check your phone in bed.
- ★ **Scheduled breaks:** Set alarms or reminders to take regular breaks from screens during workdays or study sessions. Use these breaks to stretch, hydrate, or take a short walk.
    - **CUE:** If you're aiming to take walks, place your walking shoes in a visible spot by your desk. Visual cues will serve as additional reminders to get up and move when your alarm goes off.
- ★ **Screen-free zones:** Establish certain areas in your home, like the dining room or bedroom, as screen-free zones to encourage more face-to-face interactions and relaxation without screens.
- ★ **Reading list:** Keep a list of books or magazines you want to read next to your favorite relaxation spot. When you feel the urge to check your phone, grab a book instead.
- ★ **Mindfulness reminders:** You can leave a small notebook or gratitude journal out in your workspace, or even set your favorite mug out in plain view. These little visual cues can serve as gentle reminders to pause, breathe, and be present, even before your app sends a notification.
- ★ **Phone-free activities:** Create intentional screen-free moments by scheduling offline activities.
    - **CUE:** Set up cues like leaving your journal open on your nightstand, placing your book where you can see it, or setting a reminder on your phone to shut off for 20 minutes of mindful teatime. These small prompts encourage you to step away from screens and indulge in nurturing, restorative practices.

Goals vs. Systems:
The Hourly-Reset Game-Changer

Instead of setting just one big goal, break it into smaller hourly habits. Goals are like a flashy headline (for example, "Reduce screen time by 50 percent!"). They sound great, but they don't do the heavy lifting. That's where systems come in. Systems are the behind-the-scenes magic that gets the job done, like your personal GPS guiding you through tiny, manageable steps every day until you reach that goal.

Goal Example: I want to reduce my screen time by 50 percent.

System Ideas: Use your phone's built-in settings to set daily limits for specific apps, or schedule phone-free hours (like when you're having your morning coffee or during your evening wind-down).

Goal Example: I want to spend less than 1 hour per day on social media.

System Ideas: Create a reward system and check social media only after completing a task or goal (e.g., working out, finishing a project, etc.). Or move social-media apps to a hidden folder. Place them on the last page of your phone or within a folder titled "Do I Need This?" to make accessing them less impulsive.

Goal Example: I want to limit my phone usage to essential tasks only.

System Ideas: Create a priority list for your phone usage. Write down what qualifies as essential tasks (e.g., responding to work emails, using navigation, scheduling, etc.) and stick to those. Or use a physical planner or notebook. Replace digital tools like calendars and to-do lists with analog versions to reduce the need for your phone.

Goal Example: I want to have screen-free mornings.

System Ideas: Establish a checklist for your morning routine. Write out your ideal screen-free morning routine (e.g., water the garden, journal, make tea) and keep it visible as a guide to start your day without screens. Or create a morning playlist; play calming music or a podcast through a smart speaker to help you ease into your morning without needing to touch your phone.

Goal Example: I want to avoid using my phone during meals.

System Ideas: Create a no-phone zone (e.g., the dining table). Visual cues can help reinforce this, such as placing a small sign, jar, or decorative item on the table as a reminder. Or try replacing the habit entirely. Keep conversation starters, a gratitude journal, or a fun tabletop game nearby to make mealtimes engaging without the need for phones.

The Three Layers of Behavioral Change

To create lasting change with your phone-usage habits, it's helpful to understand the three layers of behavioral change as outlined in *Atomic Habits* by James Clear.

1. CHANGING YOUR OUTCOMES

EXAMPLE: Reducing your screen time by 50 percent.

★ This is the result you want to achieve. It's the end goal that motivates you to take action.

2. CHANGING YOUR PROCESS

EXAMPLE: Implementing new routines and systems that promote healthier phone use.

★ This involves the habits and actions you take to reach your desired outcome. For instance, setting app limits, establishing phone-free times, and creating structured routines.

3. CHANGING YOUR IDENTITY

EXAMPLE: Embracing the identity of someone who values mindfulness and intentional living.

★ This is the deepest level of change. It involves shifting your self-perception and aligning your habits with the person you want to become. When you see yourself as someone who prioritizes real-life connections and self-care, your behaviors naturally follow suit.

By focusing on these three layers of change, you can build a strong foundation for reducing screen time and developing healthier phone habits. Remember, the goal is to create systems that make continuous small improvements, ultimately leading to significant, lasting changes in your behavior and lifestyle.

Reflection Activity

Reflect on your phone-usage habits through the lens of the three layers of behavioral change, using the following steps.

1. OUTCOME

What specific result do you want to achieve with your phone usage? *(Example: Reducing screen time by 50 percent, or checking social media only once in the morning and once at night.)*

Exercise: Write down a clear, measurable outcome you'd like to accomplish. How will you know you've succeeded? *(Example: "I want to cut my screen time to 3 hours a day by the end of next month.")*

2. PROCESS

What routines or systems will you implement to help you reach that outcome? *(Example: Setting app limits, scheduling phone-free times, using a dedicated phone zone during certain hours.)*

Exercise: List 3 habits or routines that will support this goal. What can you change in your daily process to make healthier phone use easier? *(Examples: Set app timers on social media to restrict usage to 30 minutes daily. Use a phone-free basket after 8 p.m. every night. Plan for one day per week as a screen-free day, like Sundays.)*

3. IDENTITY

Who do you want to become through these changes?
(Example: A person who prioritizes mindfulness, someone who values quality time with loved ones over screen time.)

Exercise: Describe the type of person who embodies the habits you want to develop. How will embracing this identity influence your behaviors? *(Examples: "I want to become someone who is present in the moment, not constantly distracted by notifications." "I want to be a person who reads more books and spends more time outdoors.")*

Habit Stacking: The Formula

The habit stacking formula is this: "After [current habit], I will [new habit]."

For example: "After I take off my work shoes, I will immediately change into my workout clothes." This allows you to take advantage of the natural momentum that comes from one behavior leading to the next.

Habit stacking harnesses the power of your current habits to create new ones by linking a new behavior to an existing one. This concept, known as the "Diderot effect," observes that obtaining a new possession often creates a spiral of consumption, leading to the purchasing of more new things. Similarly, once you start a new habit, it can trigger a chain reaction, making it easier to adopt other positive behaviors.

By using habit stacking, you can easily incorporate new habits into your routine without disrupting your existing flow. Here are some examples of how to apply habit stacking to reduce screen time and promote healthier phone use:

1. After I wake up, I will have breakfast and leave my phone charging.
2. After I finish my morning coffee, I will go outside and water my plants.
3. After I eat lunch, I will take a 10-minute walk.
4. After I brush my teeth at night, I will plan the next day.
5. After I finish dinner, I will spend 10 minutes reading a book or listening to a podcast instead of checking social media.
6. When I change into my comfy clothes after work, I will call a friend or family member instead of scrolling on social media.

Environmental Influence on Habits

Think of habits as houseplants–they thrive in the right environment. If your bedroom is a TV jungle, it's tough for an early bedtime to take root. But when you switch up your surroundings, you leave behind those old triggers, giving new habits a chance to grow uninterrupted. Changing your environment can significantly impact your ability to adopt new habits. When you enter a new space, your usual triggers and cues are no longer present, making it easier to establish new routines without falling back into old patterns.

Curating Spaces for Better Habits

Bedtime routine reset: Transform your bedroom into a sleep sanctuary by removing electronics and adding calming elements like soft lighting, a white-noise machine, or a book on your nightstand. By changing your bedroom environment, you're setting the stage for a more restful sleep and breaking the habit of late-night phone usage.

Productivity workspace setup: Set aside a specific desk or workspace that's free from distractions like your phone or tablet. Keep only your essential work materials on the desk, perhaps adding a plant or inspirational quotes, to create an environment that fosters focus and productivity.

Mindfulness garden: If you have outdoor space, create a small garden or a meditation spot. Even a few plants or a chair with a nice view can transform your environment into a peaceful space for relaxation and mindfulness, which helps you break the habit of constant digital engagement.

Closing Shift: An Hourly Check-In for Your Day

A closing shift is a small but powerful nightly routine that helps you prepare for the next day and creates a sense of closure before bed. It doesn't have to be a once-a-day ritual—it can be hourly, too. Instead of just resetting at night, try adding small closing shifts every few hours. This could include setting out your clothes, packing your lunch, tidying the kitchen, or organizing your work bag. Clear the mental and physical clutter so your morning feels lighter and more intentional.

Take it from someone who used to stay up until 5 a.m., waking up only when absolutely necessary. I shifted to waking up at 6 a.m., and it completely transformed my life. By the way, if you don't have a bedtime, this is your sign to establish one! Sleep plays a huge role in how we show up each day, and a consistent bedtime will make waking up earlier so much easier.

Here's how to map it out:

- ★ Identify the time you need to wake up to be ready for your first activity or commitment.
- ★ Work backward, allowing yourself at least 1 hour for a morning ritual, then determine what time you need to go to bed.
- ★ Set a consistent time for your closing shift to prepare for the next day.

Journal Workout

What time do I need to be up and ready for [specific activity]? How can I give myself an extra hour in the morning?

I wake up at ______, and I need ______ minutes to get ready. To have an hour for myself, I would need to start waking up at ______. This will allow me to arrive at ______ on time.

My current closing-shift time is ______, and my bedtime is ______. Does this rhythm truly work for me?

After working through your closing-shift calculations, see if your current bedtime and morning routines work out. If they don't, create a new action plan for your closing shift to set yourself up for success—whether it's prepping breakfast, organizing your workspace, or doing a quick tidy-up before bed. These small steps help you wake up feeling prepared and in control, ready to own your day.

____

____

____

____

____

____

____

Habit Tracker: Check In with Your Phone Resets

Use this habit tracker to log your phone use every day for the next week. The goal here isn't to be perfect but to become more aware of when and how you're using your phone. Let's see where you might want to make a few adjustments!

	Checked phone first thing		Used phone during meals		Scrolled mindlessly		Used phone in bed		Took a phone-free break	
Monday	Yes	No	Yes	No	Yes	No	Yes	No	Yes	No
Tuesday	Yes	No	Yes	No	Yes	No	Yes	No	Yes	No
Wednesday	Yes	No	Yes	No	Yes	No	Yes	No	Yes	No
Thursday	Yes	No	Yes	No	Yes	No	Yes	No	Yes	No
Friday	Yes	No	Yes	No	Yes	No	Yes	No	Yes	No
Saturday	Yes	No	Yes	No	Yes	No	Yes	No	Yes	No
Sunday	Yes	No	Yes	No	Yes	No	Yes	No	Yes	No

How to Use the Tracker

- ★ **Checked phone first thing:** Did you greet your phone before your coffee? It happens! Mark yes or no.
- ★ **Used phone during meals:** Caught yourself scrolling mid-bite? No judgment, just check yes or no.
- ★ **Scrolled mindlessly:** You know those black-hole scrolling sessions? Let's track those. Check yes or no.
- ★ **Used phone in bed:** Late-night scrolling? We've all been there. Log it here.
- ★ **Took a phone-free break:** Managed to take a break from your phone? That's a win!

Habit Tracker Reflections

Each day and at the end of the week, review your tracker. Ask yourself the following questions:

What patterns do I notice?

How do I feel when I take hourly phone-free breaks versus when I'm constantly using my phone?

What's one small hourly change I can make next week?

Exercises to Implement with Your Habit Tracker

ONE-HOUR PHONE-FREE CHALLENGE

Put your phone down for at least 1 hour and engage in an offline activity of your choice. This could be reading, cooking, exercising, or simply enjoying some quiet time. If a full hour feels like too much, start with a smaller goal—try going phone-free for 10-minute intervals every hour throughout the day.

Journal Workout

After the hour is up, write about your experience. How did you feel during the phone-free time? What challenges did you face, if any? Did you notice any differences in your mood, focus, or productivity? Reflect on how this break impacted your overall well-being.

THE HOURLY DIGITAL DETOX

Choose one evening this week to have a complete digital detox. From 6 p.m. onward, turn off all digital devices and engage in activities that do not involve screens, such as having a face-to-face conversation, playing a board game, or doing a creative hobby. To make this easier, try warming up with hourly screen-free moments during the day—set a few 10- to 15-minute phone-free blocks before diving into a full evening detox.

Journal Workout

At the end of the evening, write about your digital detox experience. What activities did you engage in? How did it feel to be completely disconnected from digital devices for several hours? Did the earlier hourly breaks help you transition into a longer detox? Reflect on how you felt before, during, and after the detox, and consider how you might incorporate regular hourly screen-free resets into your routine.

Key Takeaways

THE IMPORTANCE OF SMALL, CONSISTENT ACTIONS: Tiny changes, maintained over time, lead to significant life transformations. Think of habits like planting seeds: Nurture them consistently for big rewards.

HABIT CUES AND ENVIRONMENT DESIGN: Positive habits start with clear cues, so make them obvious in your environment, like using "breadcrumbs" to reinforce good habits (e.g., setting workout clothes by your bed to encourage morning exercise, leaving a journal on your kitchen table for daily reflections). Minimize negative cues to reduce distractions (e.g., hiding your phone or using sticky notes, low-light lamps, or a reserved charging station).

THE THREE LAYERS OF BEHAVIORAL CHANGE: 1) Outcome: The specific goal you want to achieve (e.g., reduce screen time); 2) Process: The systems and routines to achieve that outcome (e.g., phone-free zones); and 3) Identity: The person you become through these habits (e.g., mindful and present).

HABIT STACKING: Link new habits to existing ones for smooth integration (e.g., "After I wake up, I'll drink water.")

CURATING SPACES FOR BETTER HABITS: Design environments that promote healthy habits (e.g., creating a distraction-free workspace).

HABIT TRACKER: Track phone habits to identify patterns and areas for improvement (e.g., screen-free breaks).

Action Items

- Write down your desired outcome, the supporting routines, and the identity you want to embody.
- Create one habit stack (e.g., "After brushing my teeth, I'll journal for 5 minutes.")
- Write down a small habit you want to start (e.g., reading one page of a book each night), and identify a cue to trigger it (e.g., placing a book on your pillow).
- Create one "phone-free zone" in your home (e.g., no phones at the dining table), and set up a weekly reminder for a digital-detox day.
- Write a checklist for your ideal screen-free morning (e.g., make tea, journal, stretch). Place it somewhere visible.
- Plan one digital-detox evening or an intentional offline activity this week, like reading, journaling, or going for a walk. Pair it with a visual cue (e.g., placing your walking shoes by the door).

Notes

Part Two

Daily

Living with Daily Rituals

Transform your daily routines into moments of intention and connection. This chapter covers how integrating small, meaningful rituals can bring clarity, calm, and focus to your life. By grounding yourself through intentional practices, you create a rhythm that aligns with your values and fosters a sense of presence on even the busiest of days.

Explore how crafting rituals tailored to your lifestyle can turn everyday moments into opportunities for growth and mindfulness, helping you stay rooted in what truly matters.

4.

Rituals

Rituals are your own special routines; they're sparkly, bringing out the joys and moments of gratitude in life. Rituals are little habits or traditions you keep doing because they make you feel full and keep you connected to what really matters. For example, planning a morning ritual not only gets you up early but also gives you a reason to rise. A cup of tea, a workout class, a morning walk, or reading a book can start your day with a positive tone. This is about repeating those little acts that fill your day with bits of happiness and a whole lot of heart. In this chapter, we'll cover why rituals are so important and what types of rituals you can add to your daily life.

The Importance of Rituals

Rituals help ground us, offering stability and a sense of purpose. They allow us to appreciate the present moment and cultivate a deeper connection with ourselves and others. Engaging in rituals can lead to a state of flow, where we are fully immersed and enjoying our activities, enhancing our overall well-being.

One thing I genuinely look forward to is early mornings. There's no buzz of notifications demanding my attention—just me, my tea, and my Bible. It's my sacred quiet time, when I can feel the warmth of my mug, take a deep breath, and reflect on three things I'm grateful for. It's simple, but it sets the tone for my day.

I've noticed that when I skip this ritual, my day tends to feel more chaotic, like I'm constantly playing catch-up. On the flip side, starting my morning with this calm, intentional space helps me feel grounded and ready to take on the day. These little rituals may seem small, but they have a big impact on how I show up in life.

Examples of Rituals

Morning Rou-TEA-ne

Think of your tea as the warm-up act for your day. As the tea brews, let the steam work its magic, like a mini spa for your senses. Hold the mug, feel its cozy warmth, and take a deep breath—it's like a hug in a cup. Now, name three things you're grateful for, big or small (yes, that second snooze button counts!). From the smell of fresh pages in your book to the quiet hum of the morning, this simple ritual shifts your focus and sets the tone for a day that feels grounded, intentional, and a little bit lighter.

Walking Meditation

Step outside and soak it all in. Listen to the wind whispering, the birds chirping like they're having their own morning chat, and the leaves rustling like nature's background music. Try walking barefoot on the grass—it's like a natural reset button. Feel the earth beneath your feet and watch the world wake up, one peaceful moment at a time.

Understanding Rituals for Different Lifestyles

Rituals can be adapted to fit various lifestyles, from those with hectic schedules to those with plenty of free time. The key is to find rituals that bring joy, mindfulness, and a sense of grounding, regardless of how much time you have available.

Rituals for the Time Poor

For those with busy schedules, it's important to incorporate quick and simple rituals that can be seamlessly integrated into daily routines. These rituals are designed to provide moments of calm and mindfulness without requiring a significant time commitment.

Gratitude Pause

Take a moment during your day to think of three things you're grateful for.

1. ____________________

2. ____________________

3. ____________________

Purpose: Shifts your focus to positive aspects of your life, reducing stress.

How to implement: Set a reminder on your phone or use a sticky note on your desk to prompt this quick mental exercise.

Evening Wind-Down

Before bed, spend 5 minutes jotting down your thoughts and reflections to hit the refresh button on your brain, clearing your mind for a peaceful night's sleep.

Purpose: Clears your mind and prepares you for restful sleep.

Tips: Keep a journal and pen on your bedside table, and make it part of your nightly routine. Take it a step farther by using the "Monthly Observations" page in your *My Best Me Journal* to reflect on what worked, what didn't, and how you can level up next month. This exercise is a quick road map for future wins. Or try the "Mind, Body, and Soul" section as your personal check-in for balance. Life gets busy, but this space reminds you to care for yourself, one thoughtful note at a time.

Pet Pause

Spend a couple of minutes petting your dog, cat, or any furry friend. Focus on their warmth, the texture of their fur, and their calming presence. Take intentional breaks during your day to sit with your pet, even if it's just for a few minutes.

Purpose: Reduces stress and connects you to a sense of calm through your pet's affection.

Sunlight Moment

Sit in the warmth of the sun for a few minutes, either outside or by a window, feeling the light on your skin and soaking in the natural energy. Take a few moments to just be. Close your eyes, breathe, and let the sun recharge you.

Purpose: Helps you to feel present, grounded, and more connected to nature, even during a busy day.

Affirmation Moment

Stand in front of a mirror, look yourself in the eyes, and say one positive affirmation aloud. Let it set the tone for your next hour.

Purpose: Boosts confidence, reinforces self-belief, and cultivates a habit of self-compassion while setting a positive tone for the day.

Single-Task a Simple Joy

Pick one small task you enjoy, like watering plants or making your bed, and do it slowly, without multitasking. Notice the textures, smells, or sounds as you work.

Purpose: Encourages mindfulness and helps you realize that your to-do list doesn't have to be tackled all at once, but rather one step at a time.

Intentional Journaling

Dedicate a few minutes every day to journaling. Regardless of whether you're jotting down a quick thought, reflecting on your mood, or exploring a specific question, use this time to connect with yourself. (For journal prompts, turn to chapter 21.)

Purpose: Provides clarity by helping you process thoughts and feelings while creating space for self-awareness, growth, and slowing down.

Rituals for the Time Rich

For those with more flexible schedules, rituals can be more elaborate and involve activities that require a longer time commitment. These rituals allow for deeper engagement and provide a greater sense of fulfillment and relaxation.

Extended Morning Routine

Start your day with a comprehensive morning routine that includes activities like a morning walk, reading, and a healthy breakfast.

Purpose: Sets a positive tone for the day and boosts overall well-being.

How to implement: Dedicate an hour each morning to this routine, adjusting activities based on your preferences and needs.

Forest Bathing

Take a slow, mindful walk through a forest or park, allowing yourself to fully engage in nature. Listen to the rustling of leaves. Breathe in the fresh air, paying attention to your surroundings and embracing the tranquility.

Purpose: Helps reduce stress, boosts your mood, and fosters a sense of calm by immersing yourself fully in the natural world.

How to implement: Set aside time to visit a local forest, park, or green space. Leave your phone behind, and focus on using your senses to absorb the surroundings—this isn't about rushing but about soaking in the environment.

Creative Hobbies

Engage in creative activities like painting, knitting, or playing a musical instrument.

Purpose: Encourages self-expression and provides a sense of accomplishment.

How to implement: Set aside specific times during the week for these activities and create a dedicated space in your home for your hobby.

Mindful Cooking

Prepare meals mindfully, focusing on the process and enjoying each step.

Purpose: Turns cooking into a meditative activity that enhances mindfulness and enjoyment.

How to implement: Plan and prepare meals without rushing, using fresh ingredients and exploring new recipes.

Evening Reflection

Spend 30 minutes before bed reflecting on your day, practicing gratitude, and setting intentions for the next day to give your mind a calming reset before you drift off.

Purpose: Promotes mindfulness, reduces stress, and improves sleep quality.

How to implement: Create a peaceful evening environment with calming music, dim lighting, and a comfortable spot for reflection. Take it farther with the *My Best Me Journal* and use the "Let's Reflect" section to evaluate the six key areas of your life—time management, finances, social-media usage, self-care, thoughts, and your circle of people. This guided reflection helps you pinpoint what's working, what needs a tweak, and how you can level up for the month ahead.

Reflection and Self-Assessment

To understand where you stand with your rituals, complete the following self-assessment quiz.

Rituals Reflection Quiz. Rate yourself on a scale of 1 to 10 for each statement (1 = Never, 10 = Always).

1. I take time each morning for a mindfulness activity (e.g., meditation, gratitude practice).

1 2 3 4 5 6 7 8 9 10

2. I engage in a creative hobby regularly.

1 2 3 4 5 6 7 8 9 10

3. I set aside specific times for screen-free activities.

1 2 3 4 5 6 7 8 9 10

4. I take breaks during the day to reset and refocus.

1 2 3 4 5 6 7 8 9 10

5. I practice mindfulness or reflection in the evening before bed.

1 2 3 4 5 6 7 8 9 10

Scoring and Reflection

0-10: You have room for improvement with integrating rituals into your daily life. Start with simple, quick rituals that fit into your schedule.

11-20: You are somewhat engaged in rituals but could benefit from adding more or deepening your current practices.

21-30: You have a good balance of rituals in your life. Continue to refine and expand your rituals for greater fulfillment.

31-40: You are highly engaged in meaningful rituals. Share your practices with others, and explore new rituals to enhance your well-being further.

41-50: You are a ritual master, fully embracing the benefits of daily rituals. Continue your practices and inspire others to join you.

By incorporating these rituals into your life, you can create a more balanced and mindful existence, whether you have a busy schedule or ample free time.

All right, now that you've taken stock of your rituals, you've got a good idea of where you're at. Whether you're dipping your toes into the world of mindfulness or you're basically a Digital Zen Master at this point, there's always room to grow. And what better way to level up your rituals than by getting into a creative hobby? Hobbies aren't just for fun (though they are fun!)—they can also help you unwind, spark creativity, and bring a sense of calm to your day.

Key Takeaways

IMPORTANCE OF RITUALS: Rituals are meaningful routines that bring joy, gratitude, and grounding. They're not just habits; they also add a spark of mindfulness and connection to your daily life. Moreover, rituals provide stability, help you stay present, and foster a sense of purpose, leading to a state of flow and improving overall well-being.

TAILORING RITUALS TO YOUR LIFESTYLE: For the time poor, incorporate quick rituals like the Gratitude Pause, Evening Wind-Down, Pet Pause, and Sunlight Moment. For the time rich, consider longer routines like Forest Bathing, Creative Hobbies, Mindful Cooking, and Evening Reflection using the *My Best Me Journal*.

REFLECTION AND SELF-ASSESSMENT: Use the Rituals Reflection Quiz to evaluate how well rituals are integrated into your life. Adjust and deepen your rituals based on your score to achieve balance and mindfulness.

Action Items

- Choose one simple ritual (e.g., Morning Gratitude Reset) to start your day with intention.
- Whether you are time poor or time rich, tailor rituals to your lifestyle (e.g., quick rituals like the Gratitude Pause or Pet Pause, or longer activities like Forest Bathing or Creative Hobbies).
- Use the *My Best Me Journal* to reflect on six life categories: time management, finances, social media, self-care, thoughts, and relationships.
- Incorporate nature into your routine with the Walking Meditation or Sunlight Moment to feel more grounded and connected.
- Take the Rituals Reflection Quiz, and rate yourself and identify areas for improvement. Set one goal to enhance your current rituals or add a new one.
- Plan one day this week to have a screen-free activity, like Mindful Cooking or Intentional Journaling.

Notes

5.

Quiet Time

In a world that's always buzzing—whether from notifications, conversations, or background noise—quiet time has become a rare luxury. But in reality, it's not a luxury at all; it's a necessity. This chapter explores how intentional moments of silence can reset your mind, reduce stress, and help you feel more present in your daily life.

Through simple shifts like creating tech-free zones, embracing stillness, and making space for reflection, you'll learn how to integrate quiet time into your day without feeling like you have to disconnect completely. By slowing down, even for just a few moments, you'll start to notice how powerful a little peace and quiet can be.

Struggles with Quiet Time

In today's hyperconnected world, finding moments of silence and solitude has become increasingly challenging. Our lives are saturated with noise—from the nonstop hum of traffic and bustling city sounds to the constant notifications from our digital devices. This relentless noise can lead to mental clutter, making it difficult to focus, relax, or simply enjoy the present moment. The absence of quiet time often results in elevated stress levels, a sense of overwhelm, and an inability to connect with our inner selves.

Our digital habits further compound the struggle to find quiet time. We live in an era where our devices constantly demand our attention—from the ping of an incoming message to the lure of social media or the endless stream of emails. This endless engagement with technology leaves little room for stillness, making it difficult to disconnect and embrace the peace that comes with quiet moments.

Think of it like this: Society treats productivity like a never-ending hamster wheel—you hop on and keep running, hoping to stay ahead. But the idea of hopping off, even for a moment, feels like breaking some unspoken rule. Quiet time? It's often painted as laziness or a luxury for the unbothered. In truth, though, those moments of stillness are the pit stops we all need to refuel and keep the wheels turning smoothly. They're not indulgent—they're essential for keeping our mental and emotional engines from overheating. For most of us, finding quiet time means actively creating it. This might involve assigning a specific room in our home as a silent sanctuary, seeking out a secluded spot in nature, or simply turning off all devices for a period of time. These intentional acts of creating space for silence are crucial in today's fast-paced world and help to foster a sense of calm and clarity.

Examples of Quiet Time

Sacred Quiet Spaces: One of the most effective ways to embrace quiet time is by creating a sacred private space dedicated to reflection and stillness. This could be a small corner of your home, a cozy nook with a comfortable chair, or even a dedicated room set up specifically for quiet moments. Decorate this space with items that bring you comfort and peace—a soft pillow, a warm blanket, an altar with flowers and candles, or perhaps a few favorite books. The goal is to make this space inviting and tranquil, encouraging you to retreat there regularly for moments of quiet reflection.

Offline Dates: Another way to incorporate quiet time into your life is by scheduling offline dates with yourself. These are moments when you deliberately step away from screens and digital distractions to reconnect with your inner thoughts and feelings. An offline date could be as simple as listening to an entire album without any interruptions, engaging in a favorite hobby, like painting or knitting, or taking a peaceful walk in nature. These activities not only provide a break from the digital world but also help restore mental clarity and emotional balance.

Quiet Retreats: For those who find it difficult to disconnect at home, quiet retreats offer a structured escape from the noise and busyness of everyday life. Retreats like Sweden's 72-Hour Cabins are designed to provide a serene environment where you can fully unplug and recharge. These retreats typically emphasize simplicity and nature, allowing you to immerse yourself in the tranquility of your surroundings. No matter how long your retreat is, these experiences can be profoundly restorative, offering a deep sense of peace and rejuvenation.

The Reality of Constant Connectivity

In today's world, we are more connected than ever before. We check our phones first thing in the morning, or scroll through social media during meals, or always have music or a podcast playing in the background. Our lives are filled with digital noise. This constant connection, while seemingly harmless, can lead to a sense of isolation and a disconnect from the present moment.

Think about it: How often do you find yourself reaching for your phone without even thinking about it? Do you feel uneasy when there's silence, immediately filling it with music, a podcast, or the latest social-media updates? This behavior, though common, can prevent us from truly engaging with ourselves, others, and the world around us.

Are You Overconnected? A Quick Quiz

Do you check your phone first thing in the morning?	Yes	No
Do you feel anxious or uncomfortable without your phone nearby?	Yes	No
Do you listen to music or podcasts whenever you're not actively engaged in conversation or work?	Yes	No
Do you use your phone during meals, even when you're with others?	Yes	No
Do you feel the need to post about your activities on social media as soon as they occur?	Yes	No

What Your Results Say About You

Mostly Yes: You might be overconnected. It's time to take a step back and evaluate how these habits are affecting your mental well-being and your relationships.

Mostly No: You seem to have a healthier balance with technology, but there's always room to improve and make sure you're fully present in the moment.

Breaking the Cycle of Constant Connection

If you found yourself answering yes to most of the questions, no need to stress—you're far from alone. Many of us have developed these habits without even realizing it. The good news is there are simple steps you can take to start disconnecting.

Digital Detox: Try taking one full day each week to go completely offline. Use this time to reconnect with yourself, your loved ones, or nature.

Mindful Tech Use: Start by designating certain times of the day as phone-free. For example, keep your phone in another room during meals or when spending time with family and friends.

Embrace Silence: Challenge yourself to spend time in silence, either during your morning coffee or a walk in the park. Allow yourself to be fully present without the constant need for digital stimulation.

By recognizing the impact of constant connectivity on your life and taking steps to reduce it, you can create more space for meaningful connections, deeper self-reflection, and a greater appreciation for the present moment.

Mindfulness Practices and Reclaiming the Day

Mindfulness practices are essential to reclaiming your day from the grip of digital distractions. By consciously incorporating mindfulness into daily routines, you can regain control over your time and mental well-being. Check off one practice below that you'll challenge yourself with this week.

- ◯ **Savor your meals:** Resist the urge to scroll during meals. Instead, savor the flavors, textures, and smells of your food. Turn eating into a grounding practice.
- ◯ **Master single-tasking:** Multitasking is out; single-tasking is in. Focus on one thing at a time to reduce stress and boost productivity.
- ◯ **Tune in with music:** Instead of zoning out, try listening to a song with full attention. Let yourself get lost in the beat and lyrics for a few minutes—it's a refreshing mental break.
- ◯ **Check your posture:** Randomly check in with your body during the day. Adjust your posture, take a deep breath, and roll your shoulders back to relieve tension.
- ◯ **End-of-day ritual:** Create a ritual at the end of your workday to signal you're done with work and ready to relax. Light a candle or play a favorite song to transition smoothly.
- ◯ **Digital-detox break:** When you're tempted to scroll mindlessly, take 5 to 10 minutes to tidy up your phone or computer instead. Organize files, clear your inbox, or delete unnecessary pictures taking up valuable space—it's surprisingly satisfying.
- ◯ **Pause before you reply:** Before responding to an email or message, take a breath. Close your eyes, and think about your response—it keeps your communication intentional and thoughtful. If the message is triggering or causing you stress, give yourself permission to pause. Sometimes, our urgency to reply can lead to saying things we later regret.

Key Takeaways

FINDING MOMENTS OF SILENCE: In today's hyperconnected world, finding moments of silence and solitude is increasingly difficult due to constant noise from traffic, city sounds, and digital notifications.

WHY QUIET TIME MATTERS: The absence of quiet time leads to mental clutter, elevated stress levels, and a disconnect from one's inner self.

OBSTACLES FACING QUIET TIME: Society often views quiet time as unproductive or lazy, and digital habits like constantly checking phones or scrolling social media make it harder to embrace stillness.

INCORPORATING QUIET TIME: Quiet time can be created intentionally through sacred spaces, offline dates, or quiet retreats to foster peace and clarity.

Action Items

- Take the "Are You Overconnected?" quiz, and reflect on your digital habits.
- Choose one full day this week to go completely offline.
  Consider a structured escape, like a quiet retreat.
- Set specific phone-free times during the day (e.g., during meals or family time).
- Create a specific space at home for quiet reflection and stillness.
- Plan activities, like listening to music, engaging in hobbies, or walking in nature, without any digital distractions.
- Choose one mindfulness practice to incorporate into your day.
- When you catch yourself mindlessly scrolling on social media, instead switch gears and spend 5 to 10 minutes tidying up your phone or computer.

Notes

Digital Declutter

Think of your digital space like your closet—if it's overflowing with stuff you never wear, it's harder to find what you actually need, right? The same goes for our tech. Between apps, notifications, and constant scrolling, it's easy to feel like we're drowning in digital clutter. But here's the thing: Digital decluttering isn't just about tidying up—it's about redefining your relationship with technology. It's time to figure out what sparks joy (yes, we're going full Marie Kondo here) and what's just filling up space. By clearing out the unnecessary, you can finally make room for what really matters—offline moments, mental clarity, and a little more peace in your day. Ready to declutter? Let's dive into the steps!

1. Define your technology rules.

Think of your digital tools like items in your home. Some things are used every day—they have a clear purpose, they make life easier, and you'd notice right away if they were gone. Others might be more like things you've held onto just in case, or out of habit. They aren't necessarily bad—but they can quietly add clutter and take up space you didn't even realize you needed.

Your essential technologies are the ones that support your goals, your peace of mind, or your responsibilities—like your calendar, work tools, or messages from people you care about.

Everything else can be gently reassessed. Maybe it's time to take a break from certain apps, mute notifications, or even let go of the things that no longer serve you. It's not about cutting everything out—it's about creating more clarity and calm in your digital space.

2. Set operating procedures, and frame them as affirmations.

Create specific guidelines for how and when you will use particular technologies. This helps in establishing a routine that prevents mindless scrolling or overuse. Write down your rules, and place them where you'll see them daily. It always helps to curate these into affirmations that reflect the changes you're striving for, as if they've already happened. For example, instead of saying, "I will be organized with my time and technology," you might say, "I am organized with my time and technology." Why is this important? Affirmations framed in the present tense signal to your brain that these behaviors are already part of your identity. This positive reinforcement can help you build confidence and consistency in your habits, making them feel natural rather than forced. When you believe that you're already someone who is mindful and intentional with technology, your actions will begin to align with that mindset.

Examples:

"I am in control of my email habits and check them twice a day—once in the morning and once in the afternoon—to stay efficient and focused."

"I manage my emails intentionally by using my desktop, keeping my phone free from unnecessary distractions."

"I respect my boundaries by managing emails during office hours, protecting my personal time in the evenings."

"I prioritize meaningful connections by using my phone only for essential communication after 8 p.m., ensuring a restful evening."

"I honor my limits by setting screen-time boundaries, using tools that support my balanced and intentional tech habits."

3. Schedule an unfollow spree.

Time to give your digital space a refresh. Make a list of friends and accounts that genuinely inspire you—the ones that spark creativity, lift your mood, and remind you of your own potential. These are the people and pages that bring value to your life.

Head over to your feeds, and do some housekeeping—unfollow or unsubscribe from any accounts that no longer bring you joy or that drain your energy. Keep your digital space filled with positivity and inspiration, not comparison or negativity. Curate your online world with the same intention and care you'd use in real life. And for some extra inspiration, check out our community on our Instagram account @OfflineHumans, where we share digital-detox challenges and ideas to help you stay mindful. From mini detoxes to IRL events in your city, we've got you covered.

4. Implement a 30-day technology detox.

Think of this as a digital cleanse—30 days to step away from the tech that's crowding your life and to rediscover the offline things that bring you joy. Pick up a good book, go for a walk, or finally have that deep conversation with a friend. This detox is about making space for what really matters. The goal? To reset your relationship with technology for good.

★ **Identify technologies to detox from.** Start by choosing which digital distractions you're going to cut out. Maybe it's social media, those endless streaming binges, or apps that keep sucking up your time for no reason.

★ **Replace digital time with real-life activities.** Use your extra time to do things that fill your cup—read, exercise, try something creative, or spend quality time with loved ones. Real life is waiting for you!

★ **Track your experience.** Keep a journal of how you feel each day without these digital distractions. Notice any changes in your mood, productivity, or overall happiness. You might be surprised at how much lighter and more focused you feel.

5. Reintroduce technologies mindfully.

After the detox, slowly reintroduce technologies back into your life. For each one, determine its value and establish strict usage rules to ensure it doesn't overwhelm you again. Take the habit of binge watching TV shows as an example. While bingeing TV might feel great in the moment, it's like overeating—satisfying at first but often leaving you feeling regretful or drained afterward. By setting limits to the technologies you reintroduce, you keep your dopamine in check and create more balance in your routines.

★ **Evaluate each technology.** After the 30-day detox, evaluate whether you really missed the technologies you avoided. Ask yourself:

- Did my life improve without this?
- How does using this technology add value to my life?

★ **Set strict usage rules.** For technologies you decide to reintroduce, set strict guidelines to prevent them from taking over your time again. For example:

- I will use social media only on weekends or during certain hours of the day.
- I will watch only one episode of a show per day.

★ **Consider permanent elimination.** Using some technologies is similar to times when you agree to go out even though you'd rather stay in. You do it to keep everyone happy, but afterward, you feel drained and wish you'd just listened to yourself. Sometimes, the best move is to say no and stick to what feels right for you. Here are a few examples to consider:

- **Shopping apps that love to tempt you:** They make impulse buys so easy, but let's face it—those "too good to pass up" deals often lead to clutter and overspending. Saying goodbye to these apps helps you shop more intentionally and keep your budget on track.
- **Social media that sparks comparison spirals:** If certain platforms leave you feeling more energy-depleted than inspired, it might be time to let them go. Life feels lighter when you're not constantly measuring yourself against curated highlight reels.
- **Never-ending notifications from news apps:** Staying informed is important, but constant updates can feel like a mental traffic jam. Removing these apps can bring a much-needed sense of calm.
- **Overly complex productivity tools:** Some apps promise to streamline your life but end up overcomplicating things. Simplifying your tools can make your day feel smoother and less overwhelming.

6. Monitor and adjust.

Continuously review and adjust your digital habits to maintain a balance that supports your mental and emotional well-being. Reflect on your progress and make changes as needed.

- ★ **Check in regularly.** Set a regular schedule (e.g., monthly) to review your digital habits. During these check-ins, assess whether you're sticking to your rules.
- ★ **Adjust as needed.** Life changes, and so should your digital habits. Be flexible and willing to adjust your rules if you find that certain technologies are creeping back into your life or if your needs have changed.
- ★ **Reflect on progress.** Take time to reflect on the benefits you've experienced since starting your digital declutter. Are you more focused? Less stressed? More present with loved ones? Use these reflections to motivate yourself to maintain your new habits.

Think of these steps as spring-cleaning for your digital life; you're clearing out the clutter and making room for more meaningful things that truly matter. By doing so, you're not only cutting down on the stress and overwhelm of being constantly connected but also creating a more intentional and balanced relationship with technology. It's like swapping a noisy, overstuffed closet for a perfectly curated wardrobe that makes your day feel lighter and more purposeful.

Throwback Tech: Unplugging Like It's 1999

Embrace the Flip Phone: A Gentle Step Back from Digital Dependence

Consider getting a flip phone—a simple, intentional step toward breaking free from the constant pull of the internet. With a flip phone, you can still make calls and stay connected when necessary, but without the temptation of endless scrolling or mindless browsing. It's an easy transition for those wanting to ease away from the digital noise while still keeping a basic line of communication open.

By switching to a flip phone, you're setting some much-needed boundaries with the digital world, gently telling your phone, "It's not you, it's me." Suddenly, your conversations feel more focused, and you're no longer scrolling your life away. Plus, let's be honest, there's something delightfully old-school about snapping it shut, like you're saying, "That's enough for today!"

Other Offline Methods

If your goal is to reduce dependence on digital devices, an even bigger step is to start incorporating older offline methods into your daily life. This isn't about being nostalgic for the past—it's about rediscovering the joy and simplicity of doing things without the aid of constant connectivity. Here are a few ways to deliberately integrate "old-fashioned" practices into your routine.

1. SHOP AT BRICK-AND-MORTAR STORES.

Instead of ordering everything online, make the effort to visit physical stores. It's not just about supporting local businesses (though that's a great bonus); it's about the experience of being present in the world. Shopping in person allows you to see, touch, and choose items more mindfully, while also engaging with your community. Plus, it gives you a reason to leave the house and break free from the digital bubble.

2. WRITE BY HAND.

Instead of typing notes or journaling on your computer, try writing things down by hand. The act of writing on paper can help slow down your thoughts, making your reflections more deliberate and meaningful. Plus, it's satisfying seeing your words take shape on the page, and there's nothing sweeter than receiving a handwritten note from someone. It makes the gesture feel that much more personal and heartfelt.

3. LISTEN TO THE RADIO OR PLAY A RECORD.

Rather than streaming music from your phone, try tuning in to a local radio station or playing an old vinyl record—turning the dial or dropping the needle feels charmingly like stepping into a time machine! It also forces you to enjoy the music without constantly skipping tracks or getting distracted by your device.

Why This Matters

The goal of this practice isn't to reject modern technology altogether—it's about relearning some of the practices that can be more enjoyable the old-fashioned way. These simple, intentional actions help you rediscover the beauty of being offline. They encourage mindfulness, presence, and a deeper connection to your surroundings. By using old technology and embracing offline practices, you create space for more meaningful experiences that aren't mediated by screens.

Incorporating these small changes can be a powerful way to reclaim your time, attention, and focus in a world that constantly pushes us to be connected. It's about finding a balance that works for you—where technology serves your needs without dominating your life.

Key Takeaways

DIGITAL DECLUTTERING: When you tidy up your tech clutter, you redefine your relationship with technology and prioritize what truly adds value. Decluttering isn't about abandoning technology but rather creating space for a more intentional relationship with it.

EMBRACING OFFLINE PRACTICES: Switch to a flip phone, shop at brick-and-mortar stores, write by hand instead of typing, or listen to the radio or play records to reduce your dependence on constant connectivity.

30-DAY DIGITAL DETOX: Go 30 days without using tech to reset your habits, rediscover joy in offline moments, and assess which tools truly enhance your life. Reintroducing technology after the detox helps ensure you're using it mindfully, with clear boundaries to maintain balance. By simplifying your digital world, you create room for mental clarity, focus, and deeper connections with both yourself and those around you.

Action Items

- Declutter your social media by unfollowing accounts that no longer bring value or joy.
- Write down specific guidelines for when and how to use certain technologies and use affirmations to reinforce these habits.
- Choose digital distractions to eliminate for 30 days and replace that time with fulfilling offline activities.
- Reintroduce technologies mindfully and evaluate the value of each technology before bringing it back.
- Set monthly check-ins to review and tweak your digital habits.

Notes

7

Offline Days

Unplugging Without Losing Your Mind

In a world that's always online, the idea of spending an entire day offline might feel overwhelming or even impossible. But what if disconnecting wasn't about deprivation but about giving yourself space to breathe, think, and be present? This chapter explores the power of taking intentional breaks from screens, whether for an hour, a morning, or a full day.

Going offline isn't about following rigid rules—it's about reclaiming your time and attention. You'll learn how to ease into the habit of offline days, create a rhythm that works for you, and experience the benefits of reduced stress, increased creativity, and deeper connections. From small daily resets to dedicated offline rituals, this chapter will help you shift from digital overwhelm to intentional presence, without feeling like you're missing out.

A Day Spent Offline

At first glance, the idea of taking an entire day offline might feel impossible—maybe even a little crazy. Trust me, as someone who used to spend over 12 hours a day online and was constantly connected, I would have said the same. But here's the truth: Our minds need that break to disconnect and reset.

I'd like to say there are levels to disconnecting. You can choose to go offline once a week. Start as a beginner by trying an hour. Or challenge yourself more by taking a whole morning or afternoon off.

The beauty of offline days is you choose what you want to disconnect from. It can be social media, television, or anything that you feel is taking your attention away. These moments offline can be combined with offline rituals we'll discuss later in the book so you can choose what's right for you. (We visited this concept earlier, in chapter 4.)

Here are some positive impacts I've experienced from unplugging:

- ★ **More calm, less stress:** Disconnecting allows me to step back from the noise, leading to a sense of calm that feels rare in today's fast-paced world.
- ★ **Contentment:** Without the constant comparison to others' timelines, I feel more content with my own life and where I am on my journey.
- ★ **Boosted creativity:** By not being sucked into what others are doing or feeling pressured to keep up, I've unlocked a deeper well of creativity. As a creative, this has been a game-changer for me.
- ★ **More space for hobbies:** Offline time lets me spend more time on hobbies that nurture my identity. I feel proud of the new things I'm learning and the ways I'm growing.
- ★ **Richer life events:** When I look back at the year, I notice a richer portfolio of life events and meaningful meetups with friends—things that might not have happened if I hadn't made space for them.
- ★ **Offline-time cravings:** The best part? I actually find myself missing offline time because of how rejuvenating it is.

Now, I know an entire day offline can seem daunting, but starting small is key. Here are some actionable ways to ease into your first offline day.

Tech Reset: Planning Your First Offline Day

- ◯ **Choose your day.** Look at your calendar and determine a specific day of the week to start your tech reset. This could be a weekend or any day that fits your schedule. Mark down several weeks in a row to build consistency.
- ◯ **Mark it as sacred time.** Make this day nonnegotiable. Treat it like an important appointment, a day dedicated to disconnecting. With regularity, you'll start looking forward to it each week.
- ◯ **Turn off notifications.** Notifications are not your friend. Notifications can be relentless interruptions that steal your focus. Even if you don't go fully distraction-free, it's a good idea to turn off as many notifications as possible. Here's how to do it:
  - ★ Head to your phone's settings, browse through your notifications, and start disabling them one by one. Keep only the truly essential ones, like calendar alerts or text messages. Email and instant-messaging notifications may seem urgent, but most of us can live without them interrupting our day. Instead, choose just one method, like text messages, for people to reach you with anything truly time sensitive.
  - ★ When a new app asks if it can send you notifications, simply say no. Try this for a few days, maybe even a week, and notice how it changes your focus and flow.

Simple Practices for Your Offline Day

Simplify your phone's home screen.

Most smartphones are built for speed—one glance, and you're in. We often keep our most-used apps on the home screen for easy access, but that also invites constant distraction. To create a bit of breathing room, clear your home screen. Move all your app icons to another page, leaving the first screen completely blank. This creates a small visual pause every time you unlock your phone, giving you a moment to think, *Do I really want to engage with this right now?* It's a simple change that adds a helpful layer of intention before you jump into your apps.

Practice slow responses.

In our always-on world, it's easy to feel like we need to respond to messages instantly, but slowing down can create more space for focus and calm. Instead of immediately replying to every email or text, give yourself time to finish what you're doing first. This helps create more mindful moments and allows you to be fully present with the task at hand. By responding at a more deliberate pace, you'll find that your time feels more intentional and less rushed.

Tell people you're going offline.

One important step in preparing for your digital detox is letting your friends and family know you'll be offline for a day. Share your plan with them ahead of time so they're aware—this can also serve as an invitation for them to join you in embracing some tech-free time. Use whatever communication method you prefer to let them know—a quick call or a text message.

Invite guests.

Screen-free days can be a great opportunity to connect with loved ones over a meal or shared activity. Having friends or family over for a relaxed, phone-free gathering allows you to bond over meaningful conversation and shared experiences. Studies show that eating together can lower stress and boost happiness, so consider inviting people over to join you in your offline experience.

Give yourself gentle reminders.

Your first offline day may not go perfectly, and that's completely okay. You might find yourself reaching for your phone out of habit, only to realize you're supposed to be unplugged. If you slip up, don't worry—there's always next time to get it right. This journey is about gently retraining yourself to step away from screens and embrace a new rhythm of life. Be kind to yourself as you adjust to this new practice, knowing that progress is what matters most.

Experiment with Your Offline Rhythm

Offline days aren't one-size-fits-all. Some weeks might call for more frequent disconnection, like over the holidays, when you want to be fully present with family, or for special events that hold personal significance. There are also moments in life when the world feels heavy—perhaps due to global events or times of collective reflection. During those times, stepping back from digital noise can provide much-needed mental and emotional relief.

On the flip side, some weeks may be lighter, allowing for more flexibility. For example, if you're on vacation or in the middle of an exciting project, you might choose to keep your offline time short but intentional. The key is to tune in to your needs and allow your offline rituals to ebb and flow with your life.

Key Takeaways

IMPORTANCE OF OFFLINE DAYS: Offline days allow you to disconnect and recharge, reducing stress and boosting creativity.

HOW OFFLINE DAYS IMPACT YOU: Regular offline time nurtures hobbies, strengthens relationships, and fosters mindfulness.

FROM SMALL HABITS TO LONGER OFFLINE DAYS: Start with an hour each morning, and gradually build to longer screen-free periods.

OFFLINE MORNINGS: Sacred tech-free moments in the mornings allow for a peaceful start to your day.

Action Items

- Pick a day this week to unplug from screens—you choose what to unplug from (social media, TV, or any other distraction). Treat this day like an unmissable appointment for self-care, and follow the action items below. Let friends and family know about your offline day so they can adjust expectations or join in. Bonus: Plan a screen-free meal or activity with loved ones to enhance those connections.
- On the offline day you choose, disable nonessential notifications to minimize distractions and interruptions.
- Clear your home screen to create a visual pause before opening apps.
- When you receive messages or emails on your offline day, challenge yourself to respond at a slower, more thoughtful pace.
- Every morning for the next week, start your days without screens for at least the first hour. Use this time for a mindful habit or hobby.
- If you slip up and check your phone, don't stress. Acknowledge the habit and try again next time.

Notes

Part Three

Weekly

Crafting Your Ideal Week

Your weekly rhythm sets the tone for how you experience life. This section is about designing your dream days with intention—whether it's carving out time for solo recharges, diving into creative flow, or making space for meaningful social connections. By aligning your week with what truly energizes and fulfills you, you create a routine that feels both productive and joyful. Instead of simply getting through the week, you'll learn how to infuse purpose into your schedule and make time for what matters most.

8.

Curating Weekly Dream Days

We've made it to the fun part: curating your Weekly Dream Days! I'll first share my routine for inspiration, and then I'll lay out a road map to help you incorporate multiple Dream Days into your week.

My Routine

On Sundays, I use the *My Best Me Journal* to plan out my week. This includes scheduling my offline day, fun activities, work projects, and even syncing my work with my menstrual cycle. The *My Best Me Journal* is a quarterly journal that helps me organize, plan, and reflect on life's to-dos in a way that's not overwhelming. Here, I decide which days of the week will be my Dream Days—these are nonnegotiable. Be it two afternoons, a full day, or even several smaller pockets of time throughout the week, I commit to making these moments a priority.

Some people like to set consistent Dream Days, such as Fridays and Sundays, to create a weekly rhythm. Since weekends are usually not workdays it helps to coordinate when others in the world are also having their rest day. If your schedule is more fluid like mine, pick the best days for that week and commit to them in advance.

Understanding Your Dream Day

Understanding what activities bring you joy and fulfillment is the first step to crafting your ideal day. Here are some prompts to help you reflect on what makes your day truly meaningful and enjoyable.

Journal Workout

What types of Dream Days energize me the most? Think about whether you'd enjoy a solo reflection day, a social gathering, or an adventure.

What variety of Dream Days would make my week feel fulfilling? Is it a day for creativity (e.g., baking, painting, or crafting), a day for physical recharge (e.g., yoga, hiking), or a day for connecting with loved ones (e.g., hosting a nice dinner)?

What activities give me natural dopamine? Think about the simple things that make you feel alive and joyful. Examples could be journaling in the park, baking a new recipe, hosting an intimate gathering for friends, taking a long nature walk, or even learning something new, like a language or skill. Reflect on the moments in your life where you've felt energized and content. What were you doing?

If I had a completely free day with no obligations, how would I spend it? Imagine a day without any work, chores, or responsibilities. What would you choose to do with your time? Would you spend it exploring nature, indulging in a creative hobby, or connecting with loved ones? Write down the activities that immediately come to mind.

What do I often dream of doing but never seem to have the time for? Is there something you've always wanted to try but haven't gotten around to? It could be a new hobby, visiting a special place, or even just spending more time on something you love. Reflect on what you've been postponing and why it matters to you.

What kind of environment makes me feel most at peace? Do you feel your best in nature, at home, by the ocean, or in a charming café? Describe the surroundings that help you feel grounded, relaxed, and inspired. This can help you shape the environment for your dream day.

Who would I want to spend my dream day with (if anyone)? Would your ideal day be spent solo, enjoying some much-needed alone time? Or would you want to be surrounded by your favorite people? Reflect on whom (if anyone) you'd want to share this day with and why their presence is important to you.

What small rituals or moments bring me the most happiness during my day? Consider the little things that brighten your day—a morning cup of tea, the sunset, or a quiet walk. How can these rituals be woven into your dream day to make it more fulfilling?

What would make me feel accomplished or satisfied at the end of my dream day? Think about what makes you feel fulfilled. Is it the sense of completion from a creative project, the joy of learning something new, or simply the feeling of relaxation and peace? Reflect on what would leave you feeling content by the end of the day.

Crafting Your Ideal Weekly Dream Days: Dream Big, Start Small

Let's map out your perfect day, right here, right now. Think about what your ideal day would look like within your current life. No need for a massive overhaul—just a day that feels good and reflects what you've learned so far. Maybe it's waking up feeling refreshed, enjoying your morning tea without rushing, or carving out time for something that lights you up. Jot it down, and visualize what a perfect day looks like in your world.

Now, let's kick it up a notch. Picture your ultimate dream day—the one with no limits, no real-life restrictions. What does your world look like when everything is exactly how you want it to be? Where are you living? What are you doing? Who are you spending your time with? Go ahead and dream big—this is your chance to let your imagination run wild and to create your fantasy day.

Here's the best part: Pick one thing from that dream day, and bring it into your current life. You might not be strolling the streets of Rome just yet, but that doesn't mean you can't start your morning with a homemade cappuccino and pastry. It's all about taking small, joyful steps to bring a little bit of your ideal day into your reality right now. Even the tiniest change can make today feel a little more magical.

Bringing Your Dream Days to Life—Every Week

Dream Days are little oases scattered throughout your week. One perfect day sounds great, but why stop there? Sprinkle multiple mini escapes into your week—a mix of solo recharge time, creative bursts, and maybe even a splash of social connection. With Dream Days, you can curate your personal highlight reel, one Dream Day at a time.

Here's how to build your Weekly Dream Days without overcomplicating things:

Pick Your Weekly Dream Day Schedule

You don't need to plan a weeklong retreat, but committing to two to three Dream Days can transform your week. These could be full days, cozy afternoons, or a couple of intentional hours. Think about where these offline moments can fit best:

★ **Feeling drained midweek?** Slot in a Wednesday afternoon recharge.

★ **Need a slow start to your weekend?** Claim Saturday mornings for some you time.

★ **Want to wrap up your week feeling accomplished?** Make Sunday a creative reset day, or as I recently heard, "a crafter-noon."

Give Each Dream Day a Personality

No one likes a boring schedule. Give your Dream Days themes or vibes that excite you:

★ **Solo recharge:** For the introvert in you, consider journaling, yoga, or curling up with a good book.

★ **Social connection:** Host a game night, catch up with a friend over coffee, or invite loved ones for a movie marathon.

★ **Adventure:** Try that new hiking trail, take a pottery class, or explore a nearby town like a tourist.

★ **Creative flow:** Bake that recipe you've been saving, doodle in your sketchbook, or dive into a DIY project.

Keep It Playful but Intentional

Treat your Dream Days like playdates with yourself—no pressure, just joy. The key is to balance structure with spontaneity. Have a loose plan, but leave space for unexpected delights, like stumbling upon a farmers' market or finding a new favorite hiking trail.

Reflect and Adjust

At the end of the week, take a moment to reflect on your Dream Days. What felt amazing? What could be tweaked? Jot down quick notes about what worked and how you felt. Maybe you discovered that you love quiet solo mornings but crave social afternoons. Adjust as needed ... there's no wrong way to do this.

Pro tip: Start small. Even if you dedicate only 30 minutes on a busy week, it's still a win. These little pockets of joy add up, turning an ordinary week into a memorable one.

Remember, Weekly Dream Days aren't just about rest—they're about reclaiming your week, creating joy, and reconnecting with what makes you feel most alive. Think of them as your personal weekly highlight reel, one dreamy moment at a time.

Key Takeaways

WHAT ARE DREAM DAYS? These days are about carving out intentional time for yourself, from a short hour to a full day, to recharge and prioritize joy.

REFLECT ON WHAT ACTIVITIES BRING NATURAL JOY, such as journaling, baking, or exploring nature, and weave these into your Dream Day.

ENVISIONING DREAM DAYS: Think about your ideal environment, such as an inviting home, a serene nature spot, or a bustling café, to create a space that brings peace and inspiration.

START SMALL: Even if your ideal Dream Day isn't currently feasible, bring elements of it into your routine now–romanticizing your life with the little things.

DAILY RITUALS: Focus on daily rituals over long-term goals, using these moments to find satisfaction and flow in both small tasks and larger creative pursuits. Incorporate small, meaningful rituals, like enjoying a quiet tea or watching the sunrise, to add layers of fulfillment to your day.

Action Items

- Schedule at least one Dream Day this week and commit to it as nonnegotiable time for yourself. Use tools like the *My Best Me Journal* or another, simple journal to assist.

- Before your scheduled Dream Day, reflect on the following prompts:

  - What gives me natural joy?
  - What would I do on a completely free day?
  - What environment makes me feel most at peace?
  - Whom, if anyone, would I want to spend this day with?

- Incorporate answers from the above prompts into your Dream Day and identify simple rituals you can commit to, like taking a walk, brewing a favorite tea, or journaling.

- Visualize your ultimate Dream Day, then bring one element from that Dream Day into your current normal routine.

Notes

9.

Offline Dates

When was the last time you did something just for you—no agenda, no notifications buzzing in the background, no urge to document it for later? In a world that keeps us plugged in 24/7, taking time to simply exist offline can feel like a lost art. But what if the best moments aren't the ones we share, but the ones we fully experience?

This chapter is an invitation to rediscover the joy of offline dates—intentional moments where you step away from the digital noise and reconnect with yourself. Whether you're craving stillness, creativity, or a little adventure, you'll find ideas that help you pause, unplug, and enjoy your own company in ways that feel refreshing and restorative.

Think of this as your guide to spending time offline in ways that genuinely fill your cup, from simple pleasures to self-care rituals. Let's dive in.

A Breath of Fresh Air for Your Soul

Let's face it: Our lives have become a bit too plugged in. We're constantly bouncing between apps, notifications, and social-media feeds, much like Hannah Montana trying to balance her double life. But what if you could take a break from it all, just for a little while, and reconnect with something that doesn't require a Wi-Fi signal?

Enter the concept of "offline dates," your chance to spend time with yourself without the digital noise. Think of it as an "artist date," a term coined by Julia Cameron in *The Artist's Way*. These dates are moments when you show up for yourself, engage in an activity that nourishes your creativity, and rediscover your inner spark. No pressure, no to-do lists—just you doing something that makes your heart happy.

Julia Cameron swears by artist dates for a reason: They train us to take risks on our own behalf. They remind us that creativity doesn't need an audience. It's about just you, doing something you love for the pure joy of it. Offline dates work the same way. They help us break free from the constant stimuli of our screens and reconnect with our deeper selves.

So what do these offline dates look like? It could be as simple as listening to one side of an album, start to finish, without distractions. Just sit there and let the music wash over you, noticing how even 20 minutes of intentional listening can refresh your spirit. Or maybe it's taking a slow walk through your neighborhood, no phone in hand, just soaking in the sights, sounds, and smells around you.

Offline dates can be mini artist dates—little pockets of time where you pause the noise and allow space for creativity, reflection, and insight. They don't have to be grand or time-consuming. The key is that they're just for you, giving you the chance to connect with your true self, away from the constant demands of your online life.

Remember, even Hannah Montana had to step away from the spotlight now and then. So why not take a cue from her, and create a few offline moments for yourself? You might be surprised by what you discover when you give yourself the gift of a little uninterrupted time.

Offline Solo Dates

In need of some me time? These offline date ideas focus on your reconnecting with yourself and embracing solo adventures. Whether you're craving quiet reflection or seeking creative expression, this section will inspire you to indulge in meaningful offline experiences. Skip to the activities that resonate with you, and get ready to enjoy your own company like never before!

- ★ **Mindful moments:** If you're craving quiet reflection or a bit of stillness, these activities focus on bringing mindfulness into your everyday life.
- ★ **Creative expressions:** Tap into your inner artist with activities that encourage creative expression.
- ★ **Outdoor escapes:** These ideas will help you embrace the beauty of the outdoors and disconnect from screens.
- ★ **Self-care rituals:** Nurture yourself with these offline self-care rituals.
- ★ **Simple pleasures:** Sometimes, the simplest activities bring the most joy.
- ★ **No-spend adventures:** Opt for offline activities that won't break the bank.
- ★ **Treat-yourself experiences:** Indulge in experiences that make you feel special and that celebrate and reward you.

Self-Care Pamper Day

Treat yourself to an offline solo date dedicated to self-care and relaxation. Turn off your phone, light some candles, and create a spa-like atmosphere right at home. This is your time to unwind, recharge, and focus on nurturing yourself.

Start with a warm bath or shower, using your favorite bath salts or essential oils. Follow it up with a DIY face mask, a soothing skincare routine, or even a mani-pedi. Don't forget to indulge in a comfy robe, some soft music, and a good book or magazine.

Sunset Watching

I'll take any opportunity to romanticize my life, and watching the sunset is one of the simplest yet most magical ways to do just that. Find a nice spot—whether it's a beach, a park, or even your own backyard—sit back, and watch the sky transform into a canvas of colors.

This is a moment to simply be present, soak in the beauty, and appreciate the world around you. No phones, no distractions—just you and the sun setting on another day. It's a reminder that even the simplest moments can feel extraordinary when you take the time to enjoy them fully.

Walks

Let's talk about walks. Something as simple as taking the dog out can easily become a ritual, but only if you bring the right mindset to it. Here's the thing: Attention, intention, and repetition are the keys to turning any routine into a meaningful ritual.

You might walk your dog multiple times a day, so you've got the repetition part down. But if you're glued to your phone the whole time, are you really present? Are you truly paying attention to your pup, the fresh air, or the world around you? Without that focus, it's just another task, not a ritual.

The same goes for other routines. Maybe you read every night before bed, but if there's no specific intention behind it, it's just a habit, not a ritual that nurtures your mind or soul. To make it a practice, you need to be fully present and purposeful.

So the next time you head out for a walk, leave your phone behind (or at least in your pocket). Notice the rhythm of your steps, the way your dog moves, the feel of the breeze. Set an intention for that time—maybe clearing your mind, reconnecting with your surroundings, or simply enjoying the moment. That's when a walk becomes more than just exercise for your dog—it becomes a ritual that feeds your well-being.

By bringing intention and attention to even the most ordinary parts of your day, you transform routines into rituals that ground you in the present and nourish your offline life.

Challenge: Do Something That Makes You Happy Every Day!

Let's be real—life can get pretty hectic. But what if I told you that taking just a few minutes a day to do something that genuinely makes you happy could change everything? I'm not talking about grand, life-altering stuff here. Think of it more like your own little "treat yo' self" moment.

Picture this: You grab your favorite book, find a quiet, shady spot, and just read. Or maybe you're more of a "watch the sunset at the beach" type of person—totally valid and totally dreamy. The point is, it's about those little things that make your heart do a happy dance.

So, here's the challenge: Every day, do something that makes you smile—something that takes you offline and into the moment. Try it for a week. From a picnic in the park, to a quiet morning of painting, to simply soaking in the calm of nature, these mini moments of joy will add up. Who knows? You might even find yourself looking forward to this daily dose of happiness as your favorite part of the day.

Activities That Embrace Dolce Far Niente

In chapter 1, we explored the Italian phrase "dolce far niente," which translates to "the sweetness of doing nothing." This concept is so much more than just lounging around. It's about savoring the art of simply being without the pressure to be productive or achieve something. In a world that constantly pushes us to do more and be more, dolce far niente invites us to slow down, disconnect, and enjoy life's quiet moments. Below are some activities you can try that embrace this Italian concept.

Strolling in the Park

One of the simplest ways to practice dolce far niente is to take a slow, leisurely walk through the park. No destination, no timeline—just wander and enjoy the sights and sounds around you. Let your mind drift as you stroll, noticing the trees, the breeze, and maybe even the sound of birds. It's about being present in the moment and allowing your thoughts to float by without attaching to them.

Sitting on the Grass

Find a quiet spot on the grass, sit down, and do nothing. Feel the grass beneath you, watch the clouds drift by, or close your eyes and soak in the warmth of the sun. This is your time to simply be. You don't need to meditate, plan, or even think. Just enjoy the stillness and the act of resting in nature's embrace.

Browsing a Bookstore

If you find that doing absolutely nothing is too quiet for your mind, try a gentler form of disconnecting: browsing through a bookstore. Wander through the aisles, flip through some titles, and enjoy the atmosphere. You don't need to buy anything or read a full page. The act of browsing, free from any expectations, can be a delightful way to unwind.

People Watching at a Café

Find a cute café, order your favorite drink, and sit back and watch the world go by. No need to scroll through your phone or catch up on emails—just observe. Watch people pass by, notice the small details around you, and allow yourself to enjoy the moment of doing nothing.

Gazing Out a Window

This one is as simple as it gets. Find a comfortable spot near a window, and simply gaze outside. Watch the world move, the light change, or the rain fall. There's no need to analyze anything—just let your mind wander and appreciate the act of being still.

Practicing dolce far niente isn't about achieving something; it's about savoring the moments when you're not. It's a reminder that life doesn't always have to be a constant hustle and that, sometimes, the most meaningful moments are the ones when we allow ourselves to just be.

Tie Sacred Mornings into a Weekly Flow

Sacred mornings don't have to exist in isolation–they can be part of a greater weekly rhythm. To truly embrace the offline lifestyle, try stacking multiple screen-free rituals throughout your week.

- ★ **Morning ritual stack:** Dedicate three or four mornings per week to tech-free habits. Use this time to journal, meditate, or prep a nourishing breakfast. Keep it consistent so it becomes a natural part of your weekly routine.
- ★ **Midweek reset:** Add a midweek evening where you completely unplug–take a long bath, plan a creative project, or enjoy an uninterrupted dinner with loved ones.
- ★ **Weekend offline challenge:** Choose one weekend day to disconnect from social media entirely. Spend that time outdoors, visit a local market, or reconnect with hobbies, like baking or painting.

By creating a weekly rhythm of screen-free moments, you'll notice a greater sense of balance and intention. Each offline moment will feel less like a one-off challenge and more like an integrated part of your week, nurturing both your mental space and your sense of presence.

Midweek vs. Weekend Disconnection

Midweek disconnection offers a much-needed pause during the busiest part of our schedules. With work, meetings, and endless to-dos piling up, midweek screen-free time allows for moments of decompression when our mental load is at its peak. For example, I've found that I'm more likely to stick to my health goals–like preparing a nourishing dinner or fitting in an evening walk–because I crave routine and structure to counterbalance the weekday chaos. These moments of intentional offline time help restore clarity, reduce stress, and boost productivity for the remainder of the week.

In contrast, weekend offline days feel more indulgent. Without the demands of work, you can fully lean into rest and creativity. Whether you're immersing yourself in a good book, trying a new recipe, or catching up on hobbies, weekend disconnects help you recharge in a deeper way, offering space to reflect and connect with loved ones. Both midweek and weekend offline rituals provide unique benefits–one helps manage the hustle, while the other restores energy and joy.

Offline Solo Date: Time Bucket Exercise

Think of your life in terms of "time buckets" (not to be confused with "Life Time Buckets" covered in chapter 19!)–specific blocks of time dedicated to doing the things that bring you joy. These are the moments where you fully disconnect from the digital world and immerse yourself in activities that recharge your spirit. This exercise is about rediscovering those things that light you up and making time for them, one bucket at a time.

Journal Workout

Step 1: List what you love.
Start by listing twenty things you genuinely enjoy doing. These could be anything, big or small. Think of activities like rock climbing, roller-skating, baking, reading poetry, riding a bike, or going for a walk. Write down anything that makes you feel happy, free, or connected to yourself.

Step 2: Reflect on your last time.
Next to each activity, write down the last time you allowed yourself to do it. Be honest. For some things, it might have been yesterday, and for others, it could be years ago. Don't worry about the gaps in time–this is about acknowledging how life sometimes pulls us away from the things we love.

Step 3: Create your time buckets.

Now, choose a few activities from your list and create time buckets for them. This means intentionally carving out time in your schedule to do these things again. Whether you carve out an hour this weekend or a full afternoon next month, make a commitment to reconnect with these activities.

Step 4: Plan your next offline solo date.

For your next solo offline date, pick one of your listed activities. Plan a date with yourself to rediscover what brings you joy. Whether you decide to bake that pie you've been thinking about or finally go for that bike ride, make it an intentional offline moment just for you.

Step 5: Reflect and reconnect.

After your offline solo date, take a moment to reflect. How did it feel to reconnect with something you love? Did it remind you of a part of yourself that's been overlooked? Write down your thoughts and ideas about how you can make more time for these activities in the future.

This exercise helps you rediscover the activities that make you feel alive and encourages you to intentionally make space for them in your life. By turning these activities into time buckets, you give yourself permission to unplug from the digital world and focus on what truly matters—your happiness and well-being.

Key Takeaways

SIGNIFICANCE OF OFFLINE DATES: Offline dates offer chances to step away from digital noise and nourish your creativity, inspired by Julia Cameron's concept of "artist dates."

WHY OFFLINE DATES ARE EFFECTIVE: Offline moments lead to richer life experiences and meaningful connections.

MINDFUL ACTIVITIES: Listen to an album, take a slow walk, or enjoy nature without distractions.

ACTIVITIES THAT EMBRACE DOLCE FAR NIENTE: Embrace the sweetness of doing nothing by savoring simple pleasures like sitting on the grass, people watching, or gazing out a window.

Action Items

- Schedule a solo offline day or a few hours this week to disconnect from screens and engage in an activity that brings you joy.
- Create your time buckets. List twenty activities you love, reflect on when you last did them, and carve out time to enjoy them again.
- Choose an activity that embraces the art of doing nothing: take a leisurely walk, sit quietly in nature, or enjoy a simple, unhurried activity.
- Choose a daily habit, like walking or reading, and bring intention to it by fully immersing yourself in the experience, thus turning that habit into a ritual.
- Challenge yourself to disable nonessential notifications for one day this week to reduce interruptions and focus on being present.
- After your offline solo date, journal about how it felt, including insights or ideas for making more space for joy in your life.

Notes

10.

Offline Activities

Fun and Creative Ways to Unplug

Ready to take your offline days to the next level? This section offers a variety of offline-date ideas tailored to fit your unique desires and needs. Whether you're looking for peaceful solitude or a playful day with friends, there's something here for everyone. Flip through the categories that excite you most for endless offline inspiration!

Flower Walk and Craft

Take a simple walk with a twist—turn it into a creative flower-picking adventure! Grab some cardboard and sketch a little vase on it, then poke holes around the top. As you stroll, collect small flowers that catch your eye and tuck them into the holes, creating a cute, handmade flower arrangement. It's a whimsical and refreshing way to bring nature into your offline day. Perfect for bonding with your bestie or for solo reflection!

Paint Night with the Girlies: A Splash of Fun and Creativity

There's nothing quite like gathering your besties for a fun, creative evening of painting. Whether you're all budding artists or only in it for the laughs, paint night is the perfect way to relax, unwind, and bond over some brushstrokes. Set up a fun little paint station with canvases, brushes, and your favorite colors. Add some snacks, drinks, and your go-to playlist to set the mood. Don't worry about being perfect—this is about expressing yourselves and having fun together. Whether you lean toward abstract art, dreamy landscapes, or playful doodles, the memories you create will be just as vibrant as the paintings themselves.

Themed Dinners with Friends

There's something magical about gathering your friends for a themed dinner. It's more than just a meal; it's an experience that brings everyone together in a fun and creative way. Whether you're celebrating spring with a "Spring Fling" dinner or going for another seasonal or holiday-inspired theme, these get-togethers allow you to disconnect from the digital world and reconnect with the people who matter most.

Planning a themed dinner can be as simple or as elaborate as you want. Start by choosing a theme that excites you—drawing inspiration from a season, a favorite movie, or a specific color palette. From there, get creative with the decorations, food, and atmosphere. For example, a spring-themed dinner could include hanging fresh flowers around your dining space, as shown in the image, and serving bright, fresh dishes that capture the essence of the season.

The beauty of themed dinners is that they create a memorable offline experience. Instead of scrolling through your phones, you and your friends can enjoy a shared creative process, from brainstorming ideas to setting the table. It's a chance to slow down, savor good food, and celebrate each other's company—all while embracing your creative side. Plus, the effort you put into the theme makes the evening feel extra special, turning an ordinary dinner into a celebration of friendship and connection.

Journaling Brunch with the Girls

Here's your sign to plan an offline gathering with your crew, filled with laughter, meaningful conversations, and some good, old-fashioned bonding time. Invite your friends over for a wellness-focused brunch. Picture this: brunch spread, pastries galore, and a side of journaling. Think of it as your personal time to check in on goals, reflect, and reconnect–both with yourself and your besties.

The best part? It's about balance. Start with some lighthearted fun (hello, sparkly drinks!) but make time for deeper moments too. From journaling about your personal growth to planning your next offline day together, these gatherings are all about creating intentional offline moments that leave you feeling recharged and reconnected.

Bonus idea: Make this a monthly ritual. A little brunch, a little reflection, and a whole lot of heart.

Offline Activities Exercise

Write out five activities for offline days that feel like fun self-care and that excite you for the upcoming half year. Dream big—think about any classes you've been wanting to take, books you've been adding to your reading list, new hobbies, home projects, or places to visit and travel. Below are some ideas to get you started.

- ★ Take salsa classes starting in [month] at [local studio]. Create a playlist of salsa songs to use for practice at home!
- ★ Sign up for cooking classes with [loved one] at [institution]. Re-create one dish each month for friends or family.
- ★ Clear out my office and restock it with aesthetic stationery and organizing tools. Create a cozy, inspiring workspace with items like a mood board or color-coded pens.
- ★ Revamp my [social media platform] by curating a mood board with clear themes and goals. Map out content ideas and plan the first batch of revamped videos.
- ★ Take [dog name] to the dog-friendly beach in [hometown]. Make it a full adventure and pack snacks and their favorite toy.

Journal Workout

Think about all the things you've been putting off because you haven't had "enough time." Set a timer for 10 minutes, and list ten activities you enjoy. (They could be the same ones you've noted previously or entirely new ones.) For each activity, consider the following questions.

Is there a cost involved, or is it free?

Is it pricey or affordable?

Is this something to do solo or with others?

Is it related to work?

Does it involve any physical exertion?

Is the pace fast or relaxed?

Does it engage my mind, body, or spirit?

Key Takeaways

MORE THAN JUST A SCREEN BREAK: Offline activities aren't just about taking a break from screens—they're about rediscovering joy, creativity, and meaningful connections in real life.

IDEAS TO HELP YOU UNPLUG: By fully immersing yourself in experiences that bring you fulfillment, you'll find it easier to unplug more regularly. Whether it's a relaxing journaling brunch, a playful paint night, or a themed dinner with friends, these activities are designed to spark inspiration and create lasting memories.

LESS, NOT MORE: The goal here isn't to add more to your to-do list—it's to remind you how much fun life can be when you make space for the little things we often take for granted.

Action Items

- Pick one activity from this chapter that excites you and schedule a time to do it in the next month.
- Plan a social offline gathering, whether it's a themed dinner, a creative night, or a journaling brunch with friends.
- Create a list of five offline activities you'd love to try in the next 6 months. Write them down and challenge yourself to do at least three.
- Turn an everyday habit into a ritual. Whether it's going on mindful walks, painting for fun, or journaling, bring intention to something small that makes your offline life more fulfilling.
- Share your experience. After trying one of these activities, reflect on how it felt to unplug and connect with yourself or others.

Notes

11.

Offline Crafts

Creative Projects to Spark Joy

We're about to get crafty and embrace our inner artist! Whether you're into DIY projects or handmade crafts or simply love creating beautiful things with your hands, you'll find endless inspiration here. Whether you choose to design stickers or craft whimsical creations, let your imagination run wild. These ideas will guide you in making your own little pieces of magic, bringing a sprinkle of joy and creativity into your everyday life.

Ready to get your hands messy? Let's look at the world of DIYs that add fun and creativity to your offline time.

Resin-Art Phone Cases

Resin-art phone cases are a fun and creative way to turn your phone into a personalized piece of art. This simple DIY project lets you take your favorite trinkets—like charms, pressed flowers, glitter, or tiny keepsakes—and embed them in a clear phone case using resin. The resin hardens into a glossy, protective finish, sealing your unique design.

Clay Fridge Magnets

DIY clay fridge magnets are a fun way to add a touch of personality to your kitchen. Shape air-dry or oven-bake clay into tiny charms—like fruit, animals, or abstract designs—then paint them and add a magnet to the back.

These little magnets help brighten up your fridge and make practical art for holding notes or photos. It's a simple offline project that brings creativity and joy to your everyday space.

Flower Printing

Imagine wearing a piece of your garden—literally. Flower printing is a hands-on offline craft that lets you transfer the beauty of flowers and leaves directly onto your clothes or other fabric. It's a little bit of nature, a little bit of creativity, and a whole lot of magic.

Here's the gist: To make the colors stick, start by soaking your cotton, linen, or hemp fabric in a mixture of 1 part soy milk and 2 parts water. After soaking and drying it a few times, your fabric is ready to become your canvas. Pick flowers that transfer pigment well—cosmos, marigolds, pansies, and even carrot flowers work great. Lay your flowers on the fabric, cover with another piece of fabric, and gently hammer away to release their vibrant pigments. Once you've removed the plant material, a quick press with an iron will set the colors, turning your fabric into a wearable piece of art.

This isn't just about making pretty clothes—it's about slowing down, getting your hands dirty (in the best way), and connecting with nature. Whether you're printing on a shirt, a scarf, or a pillowcase, this craft lets you bring a bit of the outdoors into your everyday life. So, why not create something that feels uniquely you, straight from your garden?

Floral Frame

This DIY is a fun and creative way to display your favorite memories! I used a float frame, took polaroids with black-and-white film, and glued on dried florals. You can press your own flowers, collect them from nature, or use a mix of both for a personalized touch. This craft lets you slow down, enjoy the process, and create a beautiful piece of art that brings a little bit of nature indoors.

Whether you're looking for a weekend project or a peaceful way to spend an afternoon, this floral frame is the perfect offline activity that blends creativity with a bit of nostalgia.

Scrapbook Night

It's time to take those hundreds (or maybe thousands) of photos sitting in your camera roll and bring them to life in a scrapbook, turning your digital memories into tangible keepsakes. Gather your favorite moments—vacations, special events, or everyday snapshots—and print them out. Then grab some scissors, glue, and fun stickers to start crafting your personalized memory book.

This is the perfect offline activity to relive your favorite memories while also expressing your creativity. Whether you're doing it solo for some peaceful me time or inviting friends over for a scrapbook night, it's a wonderful way to unplug, connect with your memories, and create something beautiful.

Notes

12.

Offline Nature

Healing and Reconnecting with the Outdoors

This section is dedicated to the peaceful, grounding power of nature. Whether you're taking a forest bath, strolling through a local park, or spending time under the open sky, immersing yourself in the natural world can recharge your spirit. Nature offers a soothing escape from the digital noise and helps you reconnect with your true self. Here, you'll find ideas for outdoor activities that invite you to slow down, breathe deeply, and embrace the simple beauty of the natural world around you. Get ready to experience the restorative magic of nature!

Shadow Tracing with Nature

This creative exercise invites you to step away from the digital noise and embrace the peaceful simplicity of nature. Instead of traditional painting, which can sometimes feel overwhelming, try something different: shadow tracing. It's a mindful way to connect with both nature and your creative side, without the pressure of getting it perfect.

All you need is a flower (or any plant that catches your eye) and a bit of sunlight. Hold the flower over a blank page, and let the sun cast its shadow. Trace that shadow with a pencil to capture its unique shape. Then, using watercolors or any medium you like, bring the traced outline to life with color.

This gentle, playful activity is perfect for loosening up and allowing creativity to flow naturally. It's a reminder that art doesn't have to be perfect—it just has to be yours. By combining nature's beauty with a creative twist, you'll find that inspiration often comes from the simplest things, like a flower and its shadow on a sunny day.

Pressing Flowers and Leaves

Take a break from your screen and step outside. Gather five flowers or leaves that catch your eye. Once you've collected your finds, press them between wax paper to preserve them, and save them in this book as a reminder of the beauty you discovered offline. This light, whimsical activity isn't just about creating a keepsake; it's also about recharging your creativity and reconnecting with nature in a small but meaningful way. Sometimes, stepping away from the digital world and interacting with the natural one can open up new paths of thinking and inspire fresh ideas in your creative journey.

Rock Collecting

Have you ever thought about using a rock as a reminder to unplug from the digital world? It might sound a little unconventional, but give it a try. Head outside for a walk, and pick up five stones that catch your eye. This isn't merely about admiring nature's beauty—it's about making a conscious choice to disconnect. Each time you reach into your pocket and feel one of those stones, it's a gentle nudge to lift your head up, step away from your screen, and engage with the world around you.

These stones aren't just pretty keepsakes; they're your silent reminders to pause, breathe, and reconnect with the simple joys of life. The next time you're feeling overwhelmed by emails and notifications, let that pocketful of stones remind you to slow down and experience life beyond the digital buzz. Think of it as a mini tech detox, with your phone safely tucked away on "Do Not Disturb."

And if you're wondering *Isn't this just child's play?* then you're absolutely right! Remember the joy of collecting treasures as a kid? That curiosity and sense of discovery is what this is all about. These simple activities are your invitation to rediscover that childlike wonder and make learning fun again. So, go ahead and enjoy the process—sometimes the simplest tools can lead to the most meaningful moments.

Dopamine Menu

A dopamine menu is like a personalized happy playlist ... filled with small activities that light you up without draining your energy. Think of this as your personal feel-good tool kit for those moments when you feel stuck, overwhelmed, or in need of a reset. Instead of reaching for quick fixes that leave you feeling drained, like scrolling endlessly or bingeing snacks, you could instead consider grabbing fresh flowers to brighten your space, exploring a new café for a little adventure, taking a walk with your dog (or yourself!), setting aside time for a tea ritual, or planning your week in a way that feels calm and organized. Let's find what works for you and turn those little moments into meaningful resets.

Happy Things: **Creating Your Personal Touchstones**

Take a moment to list out the little things that bring you joy—your personal touchstones—on a piece of paper. These are the simple, everyday things that make your heart happy. It could be the feel of a smooth river rock, the sound of your favorite song, the taste of homemade bread, or the smell of freshly cut grass. Maybe it's the sight of a bright-blue sky, the comfort of a cozy blanket, or the warmth of a cup of soup.

Once you've made your list, post it somewhere you'll see it often as a gentle reminder of the things that make you smile. You might even want to draw one of these items or bring it into your space. Love the color blue? Grab a piece of blue fabric and drape it over your dresser, or use it as a backdrop for some of your favorite photos. These touchstones are small but powerful ways to reconnect with what makes you happy. So take a moment to surround yourself with these little sparks of joy, and play with how you can bring them into your daily life.

Journal Workout

Take a moment to reflect on the small joys you can add to your everyday life to make it feel a little more magical. What's one festive or joyful element from your ideal day that you can start living right now, even in the simplest way?

Protection Time Circle

This exercise will help you set boundaries and protect your energy. It's about recognizing what's important to you and being mindful of who supports you versus who drains you. Let's create a visual reminder of your boundaries.

Step 1: On the following blank page, draw a large circle. This circle represents your protected space—where your energy and well-being are safe.

Step 2: Inside the circle, write down the things that need protection right now. It could be your time, mental health, creative projects, or anything else that matters to you.

Step 3: Also inside the circle, write the names of people who support and uplift you. These are the ones who respect your boundaries and help you protect what's important.

Step 4: Outside the circle, write the names of people you need to be cautious around. These are the people who might drain your energy or make it harder to protect what's inside your circle.

Step 5: Reflect. Look at your circle. How does it feel to see your boundaries this way? Are there any changes you need to make to better protect your energy?

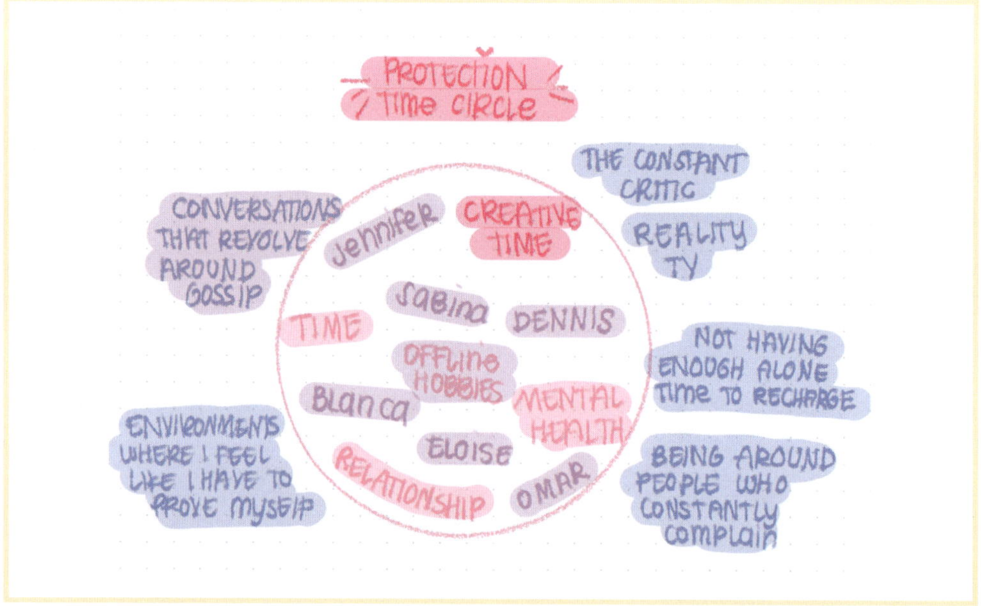

Your Protection Time Circle

Connect to Your Offline Time

Let's take a closer look at how you're spending your time and how it aligns with your offline goals. This is about reconnecting with your true desires and recognizing where your energy is going. Use these prompts to reflect on your week and to uncover how much of your time is truly your own.

Journal Workout

Where did my time go? Look back at this week and list your five major activities. How much time did you dedicate to each one? Write down the hours or rough estimates for each activity. Which ones brought you joy and fulfillment, and which ones felt like obligations?

Did I prioritize myself? Think about the activities you listed. How much of your time was spent helping others versus pursuing your own desires? Be honest—are you making space for the things that truly matter to you, or are you getting lost in the needs of others?

Did I have any outside influences? Has anyone or anything triggered doubts or second-guessing in you lately? Reflect on any moments when you've felt unsure or blocked. Were those feelings influenced by someone else's expectations or comments? Write about how these moments have impacted your choices.

Notes

Part Four

Monthly

Monthly Magic, Minus the Screens

Let's zoom out for a second and embrace the beauty of living month to month, in rhythm with the seasons. Each month brings a chance to slow down, reset, and find joy in hobbies that match the season's vibe. From cozy winter activities to festive fall celebrations, there's something special about letting the seasons guide how you spend your time.

13.

Flowing Through the Seasons

Each season is like a chapter in a story, bringing its own vibe, energy, and lessons, like distinct characters in a movie who each play a unique role in shaping our year. Winter is your introspective, sweater-loving introvert—encouraging stillness, reflection, and nights spent in. It's the perfect time to rest, recharge, and dream up plans for the year ahead. Spring, on the other hand, is your artsy, free-spirited bestie who loves fresh starts and bursts of creativity. She invites you to embrace new beginnings, plant seeds of intention, and savor the vibrant energy of nature waking up.

When summer rolls in, she's your adventurous, fun-loving friend who thrives on connection and spontaneity. This is the season to soak up the sun, lean into playfulness, and make memories that feel like the golden hour. Finally, fall steps onto the stage as your wise, grounded mentor, reminding you to harvest lessons, express gratitude, and prepare for the rhythm of slowing down.

By curating intentional moments within each season, you can embrace their unique gifts and flow with their natural rhythms. For example, winter might inspire rituals like journaling by the fire, creating vision boards, or diving into reflective books. Spring could mean setting fresh blooms on your desk, starting a creative project, or taking long walks to soak in the first warm days of the year. Summer is perfect for outdoor gatherings, beach days, or spontaneous road trips that make you feel alive. And fall encourages grounding activities like baking, organizing your space, or taking quiet moments to reflect on the year so far.

The key is to tune in to the energy of each season and let it guide you in creating rituals and traditions that help you stay present, connected, and fulfilled year-round. This chapter invites you to embrace that rhythm and craft a life where every season feels intentional and rich with meaning.

How to Approach the Seasons

Winter: A time to embrace stillness, journaling, and warm, candlelit evenings. Winter sets the tone for slowing down, reflecting, and wrapping yourself in comforting rituals, like a gentle pause before life speeds up again. Winter might symbolize the "rest and reflect" phase, where you evaluate the past year and dream about the future.

Spring: The season of new beginnings! This is your time to get playful and experiment with creativity, whether that's in the form of trying new projects, gardening, or enjoying the first warm days outdoors. Spring is the "planting" phase, where you set new intentions and start small but meaningful projects.

Summer: A season of connection and carefree fun. Picture impromptu beach trips, backyard barbecues, and moments to let loose and embrace the joy of spontaneity. Summer represents the "growth and joy" phase, when you lean into adventure, connection, and celebrating progress.

Fall: A time for gratitude, when you gather all the lessons and memories from the year and prepare to wind down. It's perfect for setting soothing traditions, like pumpkin-spiced everything, and reflecting on what you're thankful for. Fall is the "harvest" phase, a time to reflect on your growth, express gratitude, and prepare for the cycle to begin again.

Seasonal Fun with Hobbies and Celebrations

Okay, let's talk about something that gets overlooked way too often—honoring the seasons! Whether you're bundling up for winter or soaking in those summer rays, there's magic in every season, if you're willing to look for it. This chapter focuses on discovering simple joys throughout the year no matter the month, and guides you to creating your own seasonal bucket list filled with little celebrations and hobbies that make life feel just a bit more exciting.

We'll dive into ways to make each season feel like a mini holiday, from planning a vision-board night in January to a *Mamma Mia!*-inspired pool party in July. Trust me, it's more fun than it sounds—and way more rewarding than scrolling through your phone for hours.

When Seasons Shift, So Should We

You know the moment when the weather changes, and suddenly it's as if life has hit the refresh button? It may be the crisp fall air or the first warm spring day. There's something about the seasons shifting that invites us to pause and celebrate the little things. That's what this section is all about—finding the joy in marking the passage of time and embracing the unique vibe each season brings.

Here's the deal: Life is busy. Sometimes it feels like we're running on autopilot, just trying to keep up. But what if we made a conscious effort to slow down and actually celebrate the seasons? Not just the big holidays (though we love those, too), but the everyday moments that make each time of year special. From cozy winter nights to spontaneous summer picnics, we're talking about making space for fun, creativity, and connection.

Celebrating the seasons doesn't have to mean planning extravagant events or spending loads of money. It's about intentionally setting aside time to do things that bring you joy, to match the energy of the season, and to maybe bring your favorite people along for the ride. Think of it as curating a series of mini celebrations that make your year feel more intentional and a lot more fun.

In the following chapters, we'll explore how to bring that seasonal magic into your offline life, one relaxing, sun-soaked, or festive day at a time.

The Seasons as Invitations to Celebrate

How often do we actually stop and appreciate the moment we're in? Life flies by, and it's so easy to lose ourselves in the rush. But here's where the magic of the seasons comes in. Each one is like a subtle nudge, reminding us to pause, reconnect with what we love, and maybe rediscover some fun traditions or create new ones.

Now, I'm not just talking about "Instagram-worthy" moments. I'm talking about simple offline joys that make each season feel special, like snuggling up with a book and hot cocoa on a winter's night or throwing an impromptu backyard dinner party as the summer sun sets. These are the little joys that, when strung together, turn the mundane into something memorable.

Imagine kicking off the year with a vision-board night in January, when you set your intentions with friends or family over snacks and laughter. Or picture a crackling summer campfire followed by s'mores under the stars, phones nowhere in sight. There's something for everyone, whether you're into quiet nights or throwing epic themed parties.

Each season gives us a fresh opportunity to switch things up and inject a little creativity into our lives. If you're someone who thrives on social gatherings or someone who prefers more low-key vibes, there's something in this next section that will speak to you. Trust me—celebrating the seasons isn't just about filling your calendar; it's about filling your life with moments that matter.

So, get ready. The next pages are packed with ideas to inspire your own seasonal celebrations, from ringing in the new year to soaking up the last rays of summer. You'll find ways to celebrate with friends, family, or even solo—and by the time you're done, you'll be wondering why you didn't start this seasonal fun thing sooner.

Exploring the Magic of Hobbies: Finding Time for What You Love

Hobbies aren't just a way to fill your time—they're little slices of joy you sprinkle into your everyday life, mini escapes from the hustle, and a chance to pause, disconnect from tech, and connect with something offline that lights you up. Your hobbies don't have to be big or impressive, just something that brings you peace, fun, or a sense of accomplishment.

When it comes to finding hobbies, discover what makes you forget to check your phone for a few hours. The best part? You can switch things up as the seasons shift!

As the weather transitions, so too can your hobbies. From "hot girl hobbies" that let you channel your inner creative to solo activities perfect for unwinding, we've got you covered. In the following chapters, we'll go over fun, fulfilling hobbies you can visit throughout the year, broken down by month so you're never stuck wondering what to try next.

Monthly Challenges: Sparking Joy in New Ways

Do you ever get the feeling your days are starting to blur together? The same routines, the same scrolling on your phone, the same meals? Well, here's a fresh idea: monthly challenges designed to shake things up and bring a little excitement into your offline life. Think of these challenges as mini adventures—some you can tackle on your own, and others you can share with friends, building community and connection.

One of my favorites? A 72-hour phone-free challenge. Yes, you read that right: 72 whole hours without checking your notifications, scrolling through feeds, or snapping endless photos. It might sound terrifying at first, but by the end of it, you'll feel more connected to yourself and the world around you than you have in ages. It's a challenge that forces you to be present, pay attention, and rediscover what you love about life offline.

If you're more of a social butterfly, consider starting a cookbook club. (Think book club, but tastier.) Here's how it works: You and your friends pick one cookbook each month or quarter. Each person chooses a dish to make, and then you all come together for a potluck, sharing good food and even better conversation. Not only do you get to try new recipes, but you also get to create new memories—together, offline.

And, hey, if filling your monthly calendar with social events isn't your thing, don't worry. These challenges can be as personal or as shared as you like. Want to spend a month honing a new skill on your own? Try a 30-day creative challenge where you dedicate time every day to painting, writing, or learning a new instrument. Or if you want to get moving, commit to a daily-walk challenge—30 minutes every day, rain or shine, just you, your thoughts, and the world around you.

The beauty of monthly challenges is that they should fit into your life, whether you're craving connection or a little solo time. They're a way to rediscover the joy in slowing down, in creating with intention, and in making your life feel more vibrant and intentional—without the constant buzz of notifications pulling you away.

So whether you're ready to go phone-free for a weekend, commit to a new hobby, or cook up a storm with friends, incorporate monthly challenges of your own to spark that joy. And who knows? By the end of the year, you might have built some new traditions that last way beyond the challenge itself.

Challenge: Digital-Detox Weekend

Reclaim Your Time, Reconnect with Life

How many times have you caught yourself mindlessly scrolling through your phone, only to realize hours have passed? Or maybe you've felt overwhelmed by constant notifications, emails, and messages? The Digital-Detox Weekend challenge is here to help you hit pause on all of that. For one weekend each month, the goal is simple: Unplug from your digital life, and reconnect with the things that truly matter.

- ★ **Step 1: Set your boundaries.** Pick a weekend–ideally starting Friday night and going until Sunday evening–and commit to turning off all nonessential digital devices. This means no social media, no mindless web browsing, and no streaming. If you need to keep your phone on for emergencies, set it to airplane mode or "Do Not Disturb," and limit using it to essential calls or texts only.
- ★ **Step 2: Plan your offline activities.** Without your phone or laptop to fill the time, you might be wondering what to do now. This is where the fun begins. Use the weekend to do things you've been putting off or activities that help you reconnect with your offline self. Try some of these:
    - **Read a book.** Get lost in a good novel, or explore something new in your favorite genre.
    - **Go for a nature walk.** Spend time outdoors, visiting a nearby park or exploring your neighborhood. Take in the sights and sounds around you, without any distractions.
    - **Journal or reflect.** Use the time to check in with yourself. Journal about your goals, dreams, or how you're feeling in that moment.
    - **Cook or bake something new.** Find a new recipe (maybe from your cookbook club) and get creative in the kitchen.
    - **Connect with loved ones.** Plan a dinner or other gathering with friends or family–completely phone-free. Play board games, have deep conversations, and simply enjoy one another's company.
- ★ **Step 3: Embrace the discomfort.** Detoxing from your digital devices isn't easy. The first few hours might feel strange, and you might even catch yourself reaching for your phone out of habit. That's normal! But push through. The goal isn't to avoid discomfort but to embrace it and see what it can teach you. By the end of the weekend, you'll likely feel more relaxed, grounded, and recharged.
- ★ **Step 4: Reflect on the experience.** Once your detox is over, take some time to reflect. How did it feel to unplug? What did you notice about your habits or mindset over the weekend? Were there any surprises? Reflecting on your experience can help you build healthier digital habits moving forward.

Why It Matters

In today's hyperconnected world, a digital detox gives you the chance to reclaim your time and energy. It's an opportunity to slow down, refocus, and be more present in your life. Whether you choose to spend the weekend reading, exploring nature, or catching up with friends, you'll come out of this challenge feeling refreshed, more intentional, and more aware of the world around you–no screens required.

Key Takeaways

EMBRACE THE NATURAL RHYTHM OF THE SEASONS: When we lean into the changing of the seasons, we can create meaningful traditions that bring more joy, reflection, and intention into our lives.

DRAW ON EACH SEASON'S CHARACTERISTICS: Each season offers a unique opportunity, whether it's winter's quiet reflection, spring's fresh beginnings, summer's playful adventures, or fall's grounding gratitude. Rather than letting time pass in a blur, we can align our activities, hobbies, and rituals with the seasons to stay present and connected.

LEAN INTO SIMPLE SEASONAL SHIFTS: This can include activities like curling up with a journal in winter, throwing a summer gathering, or marking new beginnings in spring. Each activity can help us celebrate time instead of just moving through it.

CURATE SEASONAL MOMENTS: These help us to create a life that feels richer, more intentional, and full of simple joys year-round.

Action Items

- Create a seasonal bucket list. Write down three to five things you want to do in each season that align with its unique energy.
- Match your hobbies to the seasons. List your favorite hobbies and see which ones fit naturally into different times of the year (e.g., indoor crafts in winter, outdoor adventures in summer).
- Adopt a seasonal ritual. Choose one small ritual per season that helps you feel more connected (e.g., a winter journaling habit, a springtime morning walk).
- Plan a seasonal gathering. Whether it's a summer bonfire, a fall baking day, or a spring picnic, organize a simple get-together that celebrates the time of year.
- Reflect on seasonal shifts. At the start of each season, take a few minutes to reflect on what you want to focus on and what intentions you want to set.
- Try a seasonal challenge. Pick one challenge from the book—like a 72-hour phone-free weekend, a new hobby, or a themed dinner—to align with the current season and bring new energy into your life.

Notes

14.

Q1: The Cozy Quarter

Welcome to the first quarter of the year—the cozy months when winter is in full swing and we start thinking about fresh beginnings. The start of the year is when you should reset, dream big, and savor the quiet, slower moments winter offers. Creative projects are ideal for these colder months, giving you a chance to unwind while keeping your hands busy. Don't let the cold weather fool you—Q1 is packed with opportunities for fun, creativity, and connection. Let's explore all the comforting, crafty, and active hobbies you can try—each one guaranteed to keep your hands busy and your mind refreshed.

January: Comforting Time Inside

The beginning of a new year brings with it that fresh-start energy. It's the perfect time to gather your friends or spend solo time reflecting and setting intentions. Here are a few ideas to get the ball rolling.

Vision-Board Night

Grab some magazines, scissors, and glue, and set up a space for a vision-board night either with friends or alone. Creating a visual representation of your goals for the year is a fun and creative way to get inspired. Bonus points if you pair it with your favorite snacks or a hot-cocoa bar.

At-Home Spa Night

Treat yourself to some much-needed self-care with an at-home spa night. Light candles, put on a face mask, soak in a bath, and unwind. Invite a friend over for a mini spa retreat, or enjoy the quiet time alone with your favorite book or podcast. Don't forget to brew yourself a cup of our Ritual Tea—the Relaxing Ritual blend to unwind after a long day or the Sleepy Ritual to help you drift off to a peaceful sleep. Our dry-fruit infusions will make your self-care time feel even more luxurious.

Prayer or Reflection Board

If you're looking for something deeper, host a reflection night where you create a prayer or gratitude board. It's a great way to creatively reflect on your intentions for the year and visually map out the things you want to focus on.

Winter Knitting

Picture this: You, bundled up on the couch, working on a chunky knit scarf or a warm blanket as the snow falls outside. It's the ultimate winter vibe. Plus, it's a hobby that offers instant satisfaction, as you see your project grow with every stitch.

Diamond Art

If knitting's not your thing, give diamond art a try! It's like paint-by-numbers but with tiny, sparkly gems that form a beautiful design. It's a low-stress, calming way to tap into your creative side without needing any artistic experience. It's perfect for winter nights when you want to relax and let your mind wander.

February: Love and Friendship

As February rolls in, channel your creativity into capturing memories. This is the month for hobbies that let you create something meaningful and lasting, using your hands to bring memories to life in ways we don't often do in our digital age. And February isn't just about Valentine's Day—celebrate friendship and connection with these heartwarming activities.

Scrapbooking

We've all got endless photos sitting on our phones, but there's something special about printing them out and creating a physical album of memories. Crafting a scrapbook is a nostalgic, hands-on way to relive your favorite moments and put them together to tell a story. Each page becomes a little work of art, filled with doodles, notes, and keepsakes.

Handmade Cards

Valentine's Day doesn't just have to be about romantic love. Craft your own heartfelt cards to send to friends, family, or even yourself. You can make them as intricate or simple as you want—adding personal touches like doodles, stickers, or pressed flowers to make them extra special. It's a lovely way to show someone you care while tapping into your creative side.

Galentine's Game Night and Dessert Potluck

Call up your friends for a Galentine's Day celebration, complete with board games and a dessert potluck. Each friend brings a sweet treat for a night spent laughing, playing games, and enjoying each other's company—offline, of course!

DIY Valentine's Crafting Night

Get crafty this February with a DIY Valentine's crafting night, and make cards, personalized gifts, decorations, and more! It's a creative way to show love for your friends and family. Gather some supplies—colorful paper, markers, glitter, ribbons—and let your imagination run wild. This can be a solo activity to unwind with some quiet time, or you can turn it into a small gathering with friends. Make it even more fun by exchanging your handmade creations at the end of the night. Add a sweet touch with some heart-shaped cookies or cupcakes to complete the experience.

Book Swap and Bookmark Painting

Love reading? Gather your book-loving friends for a book swap where each person brings a favorite read to exchange. Take it a step farther and get creative by painting personalized bookmarks as keepsakes to remember the day.

March: Fresh Starts and Fun

With the first hints of spring on the horizon, March is the perfect time to get outside, refresh your mindset, and get your hands dirty—literally! These hobbies are about exploring new creative projects and getting ready for the season ahead, making the most of the early-spring energy.

Air-Dry Clay Pottery

If you've always wanted to try your hand at pottery but don't want to invest in a full setup, air-dry clay is the way to go. It's perfect for making small, functional pieces like trays, dishes, and candle holders. You can paint and customize them once they're dry to add a personal touch to your home or to gift to friends. It's a fun challenge that lets you play with textures and shapes—no kiln required!

Urban Gardening

Even if you don't have a big backyard, you can start an indoor herb garden right in your kitchen to bring a bit of nature indoors. By the time summer rolls around, you'll have fresh herbs ready for your cooking adventures. Bonus: Caring for your plants gives you a peaceful, screen-free activity that connects you to the rhythm of nature.

Spring Hike and Picnic

As the weather warms up, plan a day for a simple hike and picnic with friends or family. Pack your favorite sandwiches, grab a blanket, and spend the day enjoying the fresh air and reconnecting with nature.

Spring-Cleaning Party

Spring brings a fresh start, and what better way to kick off the season than with a fun and productive cleaning session? But here's the twist—make it a game by setting a 1-hour timer! Just like with my weekly resets, the goal here is to dive into your cleaning with focus and energy, knowing you've only got an hour on the clock. Whether you're tackling that cluttered closet or organizing your kitchen cabinets, having a set time keeps it light and fun.

Invite a few friends over to help, and make it a fun group activity. Each person can take on a different part of the house, or you could choose to tackle something together, like a seasonal wardrobe refresh, holiday decorating, or organizing a shared space. For a playful twist, you can even turn it into a friendly competition: Whoever finishes their task first or makes the most progress by the end of the hour gets a small prize (like their favorite snack or a cute plant).

Afterward, relax together with a potluck-style meal or some light refreshments—maybe even another round of Ritual Teas to keep the energy calm and refreshing. It's a productive and fun way to spend time together, making even chores feel like a celebration.

This 1-hour cleaning burst makes the task feel doable, and having friends around for support brings a sense of community to what might otherwise be a solo task. Plus, at the end of it all, you'll have a tidy space and an excuse to enjoy some well-earned relaxation.

Q1 Journal Workout:
Craft Your Own Seasonal Rituals

As we move through the first quarter of the year, it's time to reflect and plan how you want to celebrate the season. Use these journal prompts to create your own bucket list of activities, traditions, or moments of joy that will help you slow down, connect, and fully embrace the start of the year. These prompts encourage self-discovery and creativity, guiding you to build seasonal traditions that align with your unique preferences.

1. What did I learn from the past year?

2. What do I want to let go of as I enter the new year?

3. How can I embrace rest and stillness without feeling guilty?

4. How do I feel at the start of the new year? What energy do you want to bring into the next few months? Are there any habits or intentions you want to focus on this season?

5. What makes me feel relaxed and comforted during the colder months? What activities or rituals can you do to stay grounded and relaxed? Is there a winter tradition you've always wanted to start?

6. What are three ways I can celebrate the small joys of January? How can you incorporate more mindfulness and gratitude into your daily routine this month?

7. In February, how do I want to celebrate love—both for myself and for others? Is there something special you can do to show appreciation for the people in your life? How can you prioritize self-care and self-love during this time?

8. With spring on the horizon, what does "refresh" mean to me? What areas of your life need a fresh start or decluttering—physically or mentally? How can you use this season to reset your space, mindset, and habits?

9. What outdoor activities or experiences make me feel connected to nature as the weather starts to change in March? How can you plan for more time outside, whether it's going for walks, gardening, or simply enjoying fresh air?

10. What are some fun, creative traditions I could start this quarter? Is there a way to turn everyday moments—like a morning routine, a weekend activity, or a social event—into something more intentional and celebratory?

11. What do I want to remember about Q1 when it's over? What feeling or experience do you want to carry with you into the next season? How can you make sure you're celebrating the present moment, even during the quieter months?

Whether you're starting the year with fresh intentions or celebrating the love and friendships around you, Q1 offers so many chances to make meaningful memories. These offline moments encourage slowing down, being intentional, and creating small, seasonal rituals that fill your life with joy.

Next up is Q2, when the warmer weather invites more outdoor fun.

Notes

15.

Q2: Springtime Celebrations

Welcome to the second quarter of the year! As the chill of winter fades and flowers begin to bloom, it's the perfect time to embrace the outdoors, spark creativity, and make meaningful connections. From backyard barbecues to themed parties, Q2 embraces warmer weather and making time for adventure and creativity. For those looking to celebrate solo or throw a big gathering, here are some fun ideas to help you make the most of this vibrant season.

April: Creative Time Outside

April is the time to embrace nature and creativity. Get your hands dirty with some outdoor art, or simply soak up the spring vibes around you.

DIY Garden Art

Brighten up your outdoor space by painting rocks or creating little sculptures with air-dry clay. Even if you only have a small patio, adding your own personal touch with DIY art brings a sense of joy and creativity to your outdoor sanctuary.

Spring Picnic and Nature Walk

Pack up your favorite snacks or a simple lunch, grab a blanket, and head out to a local park for a spring picnic. Afterward, take a nature walk to soak in the blooming flowers and fresh greenery. This is a perfect solo activity or a fun way to spend time with friends, offline and in nature.

DIY Garden Party

Celebrate the beauty of spring by hosting a garden party in your backyard or at a local community space. Decorate with fresh flowers and set up a table for flower arranging or plant potting. You can turn it into a potluck or enjoy light snacks as you celebrate the season's growth and renewal.

April Showers Craft Night

Don't let a rainy spring evening get you down. Invite some friends over for a night of crafts. You can paint flowerpots, make candles, or try out a new DIY project. Add some comfort food and tea, and you've got the perfect offline evening indoors.

May: **Celebrations and Sunshine**

May is the month for light, crafty projects that are both fun and functional. Create something cute for yourself or make something to give as a gift. These projects will keep your hands busy and your creativity flowing.

Spring Crochet Projects

Pick up crochet projects that are lighter and more seasonal, like fun market bags for your trips to the farmers' market, flower brooches to brighten up your outfits, or cute headbands to keep your hair in check as the weather warms.

Quilting

Instead of going for the traditional quilt, consider making something a little more Pinterest-worthy. Think cute handmade makeup bags or small stationery pouches to store pens, brushes, or other everyday essentials. These are quick, fun quilting projects that allow you to get creative with fabrics and colors while making something super useful. Plus, they make great personalized gifts!

Outdoor Movie Night

As the weather warms, take movie night outside! Set up a projector in your backyard or at a local park, grab some blankets, and invite friends for an evening under the stars. You can keep it simple with snacks or turn it into a themed night with costumes and decorations that match the movie.

Floral Fantasy Crown Party

This isn't just any flower-crown workshop—it's a full-blown celebration of all things whimsical and feminine. Think fresh blooms, glitter, ribbons, and fun accessories to personalize your crown. You can set up a beautiful crafting station in your backyard or at a park and, after everyone's done creating their masterpieces, have a mini photoshoot to capture the magical vibe. To finish, enjoy light snacks and drinks while wearing your crowns for a truly whimsical experience.

Backyard Barbecue and Bonfire

As the days get longer, gather friends and family for a classic backyard barbecue. Grill your favorite spring dishes, enjoy the sunshine, and once the sun goes down, keep the fun going with a bonfire. Roast marshmallows, make s'mores, and share stories around the fire.

June: Summer Vibes and Themed Parties

As summer kicks off, it's time to embrace hands-on projects that bring creativity and practicality to life. Customize items for your home or create unique accessories to get your creative juices flowing.

Drinkware Painting

Turn plain glass mugs or wineglasses into personalized works of art. Create delicate floral designs for your summer hosting or fun, quirky patterns for everyday use, and channel your inner artist to make something both beautiful and practical.

Pinterest-Worthy Purse Charms and Trinkets

Instead of traditional jewelry, try creating purse charms or trinkets. You can customize them with pins, beads, and other little details to make each one unique. You can add variety and personality to your accessories—whether you're switching them out for different seasons or simply adding a pop of color to your favorite bag. These little pieces are perfect for gifting or accentuating your own style!

Pool Party

Whether you have access to a pool or can rent one for the day, June is the perfect time for a pool party. Keep it light and fun with pool floats, games, and refreshing drinks, and add a summer playlist to get everyone in the mood.

Mamma Mia!–Themed Potluck

Channel the vibe of a European summer with a *Mamma Mia!*–themed party. Ask everyone to bring a dish inspired by Mediterranean flavors and dress up in summery, flowy outfits. Play the movie's soundtrack in the background. We are focusing on carefree fun and celebrating the start of summer.

Forest Bathing

Step into nature and unwind with a peaceful forest-bathing session. Head to a local park, a nature reserve, or a quiet wooded area where you can immerse yourself in the calming energy of the forest. The goal is to disconnect from the digital world and mindfully connect with your surroundings. Take in the sounds, smells, and sights of nature. You can walk in silence, meditate, or simply sit and soak in the peaceful atmosphere. It's a grounding way to reconnect with nature and yourself. For a sunset option, find a spot with a view, like a rooftop, a hilly park, or an oceanside overlook. Watching the sun dip below the horizon adds a special moment of reflection and beauty to the end of your day.

Interactive Mood-Board Activity

Grab some magazines or printouts to create a mood board that captures the vibe, energy, and goals you want to bring into this season. Are you focusing on personal growth, creating more meaningful moments with friends, or simply embracing more fun and relaxation? Let your board represent your vision for Q2.

- ★ **What colors, images, or words feel like "spring" and "early summer" to you?** Find visuals that reflect how you want to feel—serene, adventurous, playful, or anything in between.
- ★ **What activities or rituals do you want to prioritize this season?** Include images or ideas that reflect the way you want to spend your time, like outdoor adventures, creative projects, or self-care moments.
- ★ **How do you want your surroundings to feel?** Think about the spaces you'll be spending time in—home, office, or nature. Add photos or objects that evoke a sense of comfort, inspiration, or refreshment.

Once your mood board is complete, use it as a visual guide to inspire your actions and decisions throughout Q2.

Q2 Journal Workout: Set Intentions

While you're curating your mood board, take some time to reflect on these journal prompts to dig deeper into what you want this season to feel like.

1. What do I want this season to represent? Is this season about new beginnings, embracing creativity, building relationships, or grounding yourself?

2. What's one area of my life that could use a refresh? Think of areas like your mindset, routines, physical space, or relationships. How can you bring fresh energy into this area?

3. How do I want to feel by the end of this quarter? Are you hoping to feel energized, accomplished, peaceful, connected? Write about the emotions you want to cultivate over the next few months.

4. What are three specific experiences I want to prioritize this season? Do you want to focus on outdoor activities, creative projects, social events, or personal goals? Think about how you want to fill your time offline.

5. What steps can I take to stay present and mindful this quarter? Consider how you can build more offline moments into your daily or weekly routine. What habits or rituals can help you stay grounded?

6. What seeds (goals, habits, or projects) do I want to plant this season? Are there any personal or professional goals you want to begin working toward? What small habits can you start now that will grow into something meaningful?

7. Where in my life do I want to invite more creativity or spontaneity? Are there areas of your routine that feel too rigid or repetitive? What's one creative outlet or activity you've been wanting to explore but haven't made time for? Is there a way to bring more playfulness into your daily life, like through music, movement, or hands-on hobbies?

8. What does a "fresh start" look like for me right now? Are there habits you want to reset or introduce–such as a new morning routine, healthier boundaries with technology, or a commitment to movement? Does your space need a refresh? Maybe decluttering, rearranging your surroundings, or adding intentional touches (like fresh flowers or new decor) to inspire a sense of renewal? What's one small, tangible action you can take this week to step into this fresh start?

Notes

16.

Q3: Golden-Hour Adventures

As the summer heat peaks and slowly cools into the first whispers of fall, Q3 is the perfect time to embrace everything this vibrant season has to offer. From outdoor parties to end-of-summer rituals, there are endless ways to have fun offline. Let's look at some creative and community-focused activities to celebrate these months.

July: Summer Celebrations and Adventures

July is about embracing the summer sun and getting outside for creative exploration. Pick up a camera and capture the beauty of the season.

DIY Flower Crowns

Head outside and gather wildflowers or fallen blooms to craft your own flower crown. You can also use store-bought or faux flowers to get the same whimsical look. This activity allows you to connect with nature hands-on without disturbing any gardens, and you'll create a beautiful accessory for fun summer photos or outdoor events.

Photography Walks

Explore your city, local parks, or nature trails with a camera in hand. Capture stunning summer sunsets, blooming flowers, or everyday moments on your photography walk as a creative way to appreciate the world around you. It's a great excuse to get out and explore new spots!

European Summer–Themed Potluck

Dreaming of the Mediterranean? Host a European Summer–themed potluck where each guest brings a dish inspired by their favorite European cuisine—fresh Italian pasta, French pastries, Greek salads, etc. Keep it casual but chic with summer linens and outdoor seating, and play European tunes in the background.

Outdoor Adventure Day

Take advantage of the long summer days by organizing an outdoor adventure, anything from hiking, kayaking, or stand-up paddleboarding to simply going on a day trip to explore a nearby park or nature reserve. Pack a picnic lunch and snacks, and enjoy a day spent offline, soaking up nature with friends or family.

Ice-Cream Social and Journal-Reflection Gathering

Host a laid-back ice-cream social with a DIY sundae bar, perfect for a meaningful and fun gathering. Set up a simple sundae station with a variety of ice-cream flavors and toppings like fresh fruit, nuts, and sauces. After enjoying your creations, transition into a relaxed journal-reflection session. Encourage guests to bring their own journals, or for a more structured experience, introduce the *My Best Me Journal*—a great tool for reflection and growth. Provide reflective prompts like "What's one new thing you want to try before the season ends?" or "What's been your favorite summer memory so far?"

August: Summer Farewells and Back-to-School Fun

As the heat of summer continues, slow down and enjoy relaxing hands-on hobbies that add a personal touch to your home decor.

Candle Making

Create your own summer-inspired candles with scents like lavender, lemon, and coconut. Not only is it relaxing, but you'll also end up with beautiful personalized candles to use on cold nights or to give as thoughtful gifts.

Pressed-Flower Art

Instead of picking flowers, collect fallen petals or leaves on your summer walks, or use flowers you've grown yourself. Press them into framed art, bookmarks, or decorative cards. This peaceful, slow-paced hobby allows you to preserve a bit of summer's beauty in a thoughtful and responsible way, creating something personal and unique.

Mia Thermopolis Slumber Party

Channel your inner princess with a Mia Thermopolis-inspired slumber party. Rewatch your favorite *Princess Diaries* movie, set up DIY makeover stations, and enjoy a night of girlie fun. Don't forget comfort food, face masks, and lots of laughs with your besties.

Outdoor Karaoke Night

Make the most of those warm summer nights by hosting an outdoor karaoke night. Set up a simple sound system in your backyard, at a park, or on a rooftop, and invite friends to belt out their favorite tunes under the stars. Create fun categories like "Throwback Hits" or "Summer Anthems" to keep the vibe lively. Decorate with string lights, offer snacks, and turn it into a fun, laid-back party to close out the summer.

Summer Night Bonfire and Stargazing

As summer starts to wind down, gather your friends for an evening bonfire and stargazing session. Toast marshmallows, share stories around the fire, and take in the beauty of the night sky. Bring blankets and pillows for ultimate comfort, and if you're into astronomy, see if you can spot constellations or shooting stars.

September: Transitioning to Fall and Reflecting

As fall approaches, it's time to shift into a more organized, productive mindset. These hobbies are perfect for setting goals, planning ahead, and getting creative with how you approach the new season.

Reset Journaling

Get ready for fall by setting up your journal with habit trackers, creative layouts, and to-do lists. The *My Best Me Journal* already has all that in one place, making it easy to align with the Best Me Reset Challenge—from setting goals to tracking habits like waking up early and staying off your phone. It's the perfect tool to help you reset and grow into the best version of yourself as the new season begins.

Bookbinding

Try your hand at making your own notebooks or sketchbooks. This craft allows you to create something entirely unique—from a blank journal for your thoughts to a sketchbook for creative doodles. It's a lovely way to craft something you can use all year long.

Sunset Picnic and Poetry Reading

As the summer sunsets start to get earlier, gather a group of friends for a sunset picnic. Bring along favorite snacks, and after eating, each person can share a poem they love or one they've written themselves. Reflect on the season, celebrate the transition into fall, and enjoy an offline evening filled with creativity.

Fall Equinox Party and Seasonal-Treat Swap

The fall equinox is the perfect time to gather friends for a low-key and meaningful party. As you celebrate the balance of day and night, host a seasonal-treat swap where each guest brings a homemade or seasonal treat that represents their energy for the upcoming season. Think along the lines of pumpkin bread, cinnamon cookies, and spiced apple muffins—anything that embodies the flavors of fall. After the swap, everyone can share why they chose their specific treat and what it means to them as they prepare for the comforting, reflective days ahead. End the evening by sharing the treats over warm drinks and good conversation, creating a sense of community as you transition into fall.

Pumpkin Painting and Mug/Book Swap

Celebrate the start of fall with a pumpkin-painting and swap night! Gather your friends, pick up some small pumpkins, and let your creativity flow. Whether you're painting spooky designs or going for a more aesthetic fall vibe with earthy tones and patterns, welcome the upcoming season and set the mood with calming music, warm drinks, and fall treats. To make the evening even more fun, include a swap:

- ★ **For a mug swap**, each guest brings a fall-themed or cute mug to trade. Whether they showcase quirky designs or classic autumn colors, it's a fun way to exchange something that adds a bit of warmth to the season. After the swap, everyone can use their new mug for hot cocoa or tea.
- ★ **For a book swap,** have everyone bring a favorite spooky or autumn-themed book to exchange. The swap offers a fun way to discover new reads and get in the seasonal spirit.

Additional Journal Prompts for Your Gatherings

Use these prompts to spark meaningful conversations during your offline gatherings or as personal reflections afterward. Unlike the Journal Workout that follows, which focuses on structured intention-setting, these prompts are designed to encourage discussion, connection, and shared insights with others.

1. What does being offline mean to you, and how has it impacted your well-being this season? Reflect on your experiences staying present and minimizing distractions. How has this practice changed your outlook?

2. What's one area of your life you'd like to focus more on for the rest of the summer? Identify something—self-care, relationships, or creativity—you want to invest more energy into.

3. What new experiences or adventures would you like to embrace before summer ends? Consider any activities, places, or challenges you've been putting off and how they can add value to your life.

4. How can you nurture your relationships over the rest of this season? Think about friends, family, and yourself. What actions can help you strengthen those connections?

5. What's a habit or routine you've let go of that you'd like to bring back? Reflect on habits that made you feel grounded or fulfilled and how you can reincorporate them into your daily life.

6. In what ways can you bring more fun and spontaneity into your life this season? Explore how you can embrace more joy and lighthearted moments as you finish the summer.

7. What's something you've learned about yourself this summer that surprised you? Think about any personal growth or realizations you've had and what they mean for your journey moving forward.

8. How do you want to feel by the end of this quarter, and what steps can you take to achieve that feeling? Set an intention for the remainder of the season, and outline actions that can help you reach that desired emotional state.

Q3 Mood-Board Activity

As summer comes to a close, pause and reflect on how you want to embrace this season. Are you planning to make the most of long, sunny days, or are you preparing for the slower, more relaxed days ahead? This mood-board activity will help you visualize your intentions for the months to come.

- ★ **Summer adventures and early-fall vibes:** Find images or words that represent the essence of Q3 for you. Think about how you want to capture the summer's energy and how you'll welcome the slower pace of fall. What outdoor activities, adventures, or social events do you want to prioritize before summer fades? What fall traditions or rituals are you excited to create as the season changes?
- ★ **Energy and growth: Focus on how you want to feel during this time.** What images, colors, or symbols represent the kind of energy you want to bring into the season? Do you feel energized and adventurous, or are you craving more rest and reflection as fall approaches?
- ★ **Reflection and letting go:** Choose visuals that represent what you need to let go of from the earlier part of the year. Use this mood board as a visual reminder of what you want to release before heading into fall. Is there a habit or mindset you're ready to let go of as the season changes? What images capture those feelings?
- ★ **Personal projects and goals:** What creative projects or personal goals do you want to focus on for the rest of summer and into early fall? Look for visuals that represent what you want to achieve, like a new skill, a creative pursuit, or a habit you're committed to maintaining.

Q3 Journal Workout: Reflect

These journal prompts will help you analyze and process your intentions for Q3.

1. What's one experience I want to prioritize before the summer ends, and how will it add value to my life? Reflect on what adventure or activity will bring you the most fulfillment before the season shifts.

2. As fall approaches, how can I create more space for rest and reflection in my daily life? Think about how you can shift gears and bring more mindfulness into your routine as the pace of life begins to slow down.

3. How can I bring more play and adventure into my life?

4. Who or what brings me the most joy, and how can I nurture that?

5. What's one fear I'd like to let go of this season?

6. What's one habit I want to establish in Q3 that will help me stay grounded during the seasonal transition? Consider what routines or practices will help you navigate the shift from summer to fall.

7. How do I want to grow during the remainder of summer? Reflect on your personal development—what areas of your life do you want to evolve or nurture over the next few months?

8. What relationships or connections do I want to invest in during Q3, and how will I do it? Think about how you can deepen your relationships and focus on building meaningful offline connections.

9. What's something I've learned about myself this summer, and how can I carry that insight into fall? Consider the lessons you've learned over the summer and how they can guide your decisions as the season shifts.

10. What's something I need to let go of from the first half of the year to make space for new growth in the fall? Reflect on any emotional or mental clutter you want to release as you move forward.

11. What does the transition from summer to fall represent for me personally? Explore how you approach this seasonal shift emotionally and mentally. Is it a time for slowing down, or does it bring new energy?

Notes

17.

Q4: Fall Festivities

As the crisp air sets in and the holiday season approaches, it's time to slow down and savor the coziness of fall through gatherings, personal reflection, or creative activities. Wind down the year and savor moments of offline connection with these thoughtful seasonal activities.

October: Fall Vibes and Spooky Fun

October brings a sense of warmth and comfort as the days get shorter and chillier. Embrace fall traditions and indulge in creative projects that celebrate the season.

Halloween Movie Marathon and Costume Party

Gather friends for a low-key Halloween movie marathon featuring classic spooky films. Make it interactive by having each guest dress up according to the theme of their favorite movie. Set up a hot-cider or hot-cocoa bar, and bring out blankets to create a relaxed and fun atmosphere.

Pumpkin-Patch Adventure and Baking Day

Head to a local pumpkin patch with friends, pick out pumpkins, and then head back home to bake fall-themed treats like pumpkin bread, pies, or cinnamon rolls. Spend the day offline enjoying the simple pleasures of fall. Share recipes and enjoy a fun afternoon baking together.

Pumpkin Carving and Potluck Dinner

Bring friends together for a classic pumpkin-carving night but with a twist—pair it with a potluck dinner! Each guest brings a dish that represents their favorite fall flavors, for instance a warm soup, homemade bread, or spiced desserts. While everyone carves their pumpkins, you can swap recipes and enjoy a delicious home-cooked meal. At the end of the night, light up the carved pumpkins for a festive photo session.

Pumpkin Decorating (Without Carving)

Instead of carving pumpkins, try decorating them with paint, glitter, or dried flowers. This no-carve approach keeps things clean while letting you get creative with colors and textures—perfect for adding a festive touch to your home.

Pine Cone Bird Feeders

Create DIY bird feeders using pine cones, peanut butter, and birdseed. Hang them outside, and enjoy watching birds come to visit. This simple, nature-inspired project brings wildlife to your yard while connecting you to the season's natural beauty.

Personalized Fall Reading Nook

Dedicate a corner of your home to creating a comfy fall reading nook. Add soft blankets, twinkle lights, and autumn-scented candles to motivate you to unwind and enjoy your favorite books throughout October.

November: Gratitude and Connection

November is the perfect time to slow down and appreciate the little things. These hobbies help you embrace the season's peaceful pace while making something comforting and personal.

Hand-Painted Mugs

Customize your own set of mugs with paint pens or ceramic markers, and decorate them with fall themes or personal touches to add a festive element to your morning coffee or tea.

Autumn Puzzle Night

Spend an evening working on an autumn-themed puzzle, paired with hot cider or tea. Unplug, relax, and focus on something calming while embracing the slower pace of the season.

Homemade Jam or Preserves

Take advantage of the season's fruits, like apples or cranberries, and make your own jam or preserves. It's a delicious hobby that brings the flavors of fall into your kitchen, and it's perfect for gifting or storing in the colder months ahead.

Friendsgiving Gratitude Circle

Host a Friendsgiving with a twist by incorporating a gratitude circle before or after the meal. Each guest shares something they are grateful for from the past year, creating a meaningful connection. Keep it cozy with a homemade dinner, warm drinks, and offline conversations focused on reflection and connection.

Board-Game and Hot-Cocoa Night

As the weather cools, invite friends over for a board-game night. Serve homemade hot cocoa or mulled cider, and let everyone bring their favorite board game, from strategy games to lighthearted fun. This is an easy, nostalgic way to enjoy a screen-free evening.

Book-Club and Blanket-Fort Night

Invite friends over for a book-club night where each person brings a book they've been reading or would like to recommend. Have each guest bring a blanket too. It'll make the fort even cozier and give everyone their own little comfort zone. Settle in with warm drinks, snacks, and good conversation. Discuss the books, share reading tips, and enjoy a playful offline evening.

Recipe Swap and Fall Baking Day

Before the holiday rush begins, gather friends for a relaxed recipe swap and baking day. Each guest brings a favorite fall recipe to share–from treasured family dishes to something new they've discovered. Spend the day baking together, chatting, and enjoying the comforting smells of the season. Everyone leaves with a new recipe to try at home.

December: **Winter Warmth and Reflection**

December brings festive joy, and these holiday-inspired hobbies will add warmth and cheer to your space. From crafting gifts to decorating your home, these activities are made for snug winter nights.

Festive Garland Making

Make a garland using popcorn, dried oranges, and cinnamon sticks. Not only does it add a calming touch to your home, but the natural scents of the season will fill the air as you work on this charming craft.

Winter Photo Album

Create a physical photo album to capture memories from your holiday season. Print out your favorite photos, add captions, and decorate the pages with festive stickers or drawings to preserve holiday moments and disconnect from the digital world.

Personalized Hot-Cocoa Kits

Assemble DIY hot-cocoa kits with fun toppings like marshmallows, peppermint sticks, and chocolate shavings. Package them in jars or cute boxes for gifting, or keep them on hand for comfy nights at home.

Holiday Light Tour and Hot-Chocolate Picnic

Plan a holiday light tour in your neighborhood or town, but instead of driving, bundle up and walk the streets with friends or family. Pack a thermos of hot chocolate and snacks for a fun walking picnic. This offline activity lets you soak in the holiday spirit while getting some fresh air.

Winter Solstice Reflection Night

Mark the longest night of the year by hosting a quiet, reflective winter solstice. Light candles or a fireplace, and invite friends over for a relaxed evening of journaling and reflection. Provide prompts to help everyone reflect on the past year and set intentions for the coming one. End the night with a quiet meditation or peaceful conversation.

DIY Holiday Ornament Party

Get creative and invite friends or family over to make DIY holiday ornaments. Gather simple materials like wood slices, ribbons, and paints, and let everyone create personalized ornaments for the season. It's a fun, creative way to spend time together and make meaningful handmade decorations.

Q4 Journal Workout: Reflect and Connect

1. What does fall symbolize for me this year, and how can I align with its energy? Reflect on what fall represents in your life right now—whether it's slowing down, letting go, or embracing change.

2. What is one thing I'm ready to release before the year ends? Think about a habit, a mindset, or a responsibility that no longer serves you. How can letting go create space for something new?

3. How can I nurture more gratitude in my daily life? As the season of Thanksgiving approaches, consider how you can build more moments of gratitude into your routine and relationships.

4. What am I most grateful for from this past year?

5. What lessons have I harvested, and how do I want to use those lessons moving forward? Reflect on the lessons, challenges, and successes of the year and how they can shape your intentions for the final months.

6. What brings me comfort and warmth during the colder months, and how can I make more time for those things? What nurtures you in the fall and winter? Is it physical comfort or emotional warmth? How can you prioritize those things that bring you comfort?

7. What's one goal or project I still want to complete before the year ends? Focus on one meaningful goal you can work on during Q4 to close out the year feeling fulfilled.

8. How can I strengthen my connections with friends or family this season? Consider ways you can invest in your relationships. Are they through quality time, thoughtful gestures, or deeper conversations?

9. What traditions, old or new, do I want to focus on this holiday season? Reflect on the traditions that bring you joy, or create new ones that align with your values and lifestyle.

10. How do I want to feel as I move into the new year? Set an emotional intention for how you want to approach the start of the new year, and think about the actions or mindset shifts that can support that feeling.

11. What are the most meaningful moments from this past year that I want to carry with me into the future? Reflect on the standout memories, accomplishments, and connections from the year. How can they continue to shape your life moving forward?

12. How can I simplify and slow down as the year ends?

Monthly Challenges

The Small-Things Bucket List: This is a collection of life's little joys–simple, quick, and easy on the wallet. It's like sprinkling in moments that make your day just a bit brighter without needing to plan an elaborate adventure. These are the things that keep you looking forward to something, no matter how small.

For example, each year, write yourself a birthday card. Yup, a little note from you to future you. Head to the store, pick out the cutest card you can find, and write something you'll look forward to reading next year. Then pop it in your scrapbook or memory box for a sweet little surprise on your next birthday.

For more inspiration, here are a few other ideas to add to your Small-Things Bucket List.

★ **Have a solo picnic in the park.** Grab a blanket, pack your favorite snacks, and enjoy some solo time outdoors–no distractions, just you and the breeze.

★ **Send a surprise postcard to a friend.** No special reason needed! Pick out a cute postcard, write something fun, and send it off to make someone's day.

★ **Try a new recipe once a month.** Pick something you've never made before and treat yourself to a mini culinary adventure right in your kitchen.

★ **Visit a bookstore and buy yourself a "just because" book.** No pressure to read it right away–just something to look forward to.

★ **Pick a flower on a walk and press it in a book.** Next time you're out for a stroll, pick a wildflower and press it between the pages of a book for a sweet keepsake for whenever you rediscover it later.

★ **Create a "Playlist of the Year, Month by Month."** At the end of each month, create a playlist of the songs that defined that month for you. Add them to a year-end playlist to create a musical time capsule you can revisit in the future. By choosing a few favorites each month, you'll capture the essence of your year in music, one moment at a time.

★ **Keep a jar of mini accomplishments.** Each time you do something you're proud of, write it down and toss it in a jar. At the end of the year, open it up and celebrate how far you've come.

★ **Collect a postcard from every place you visit.** On your next trip, pick up a postcard, jot down a favorite memory from that visit, and stash it away in a memory box. Over time, you'll have a personal travel scrapbook that captures snapshots of your journeys, one postcard at a time. It's a simple way to look back and reminisce about your adventures.

★ **Create a birthday time capsule.** Every year on your birthday, write down your favorite memories, goals, or things you're grateful for from the past year. Seal it in an envelope and open it on your birthday next year.

Action Items for Q1–Q4

- Pick a key activity for each month of the season. Choose one fun offline activity for each month—for instance, Pumpkin Carving and Potluck in October, Friendsgiving Gratitude Circle in November, and Holiday Light Tour in December. Focus on what excites you and aligns with your schedule.
- Invite friends or plan solo time. Depending on the activity, decide whether you want to invite others or enjoy a solo moment. If it's a gathering, reach out to friends or family and set a date. If it's a personal activity, block off time in your calendar to make it happen.
- Journal and reflect. Use the Q4 journal prompts to reflect on what this season means to you. Start with one prompt to guide your thoughts on how you want to close out the year.
- Create a seasonal ritual. Establish one small ritual that will help you stay grounded through Q4. It could be as simple as a weekly reflective walk, lighting candles and journaling, or a end-of-day routine to disconnect from screens and reconnect with yourself.
- Prepare for a festive gathering. If you're planning a social gathering, be it a Friendsgiving, a Halloween movie marathon, or a DIY ornament-making party, start prepping early, and create a checklist to make it stress-free and enjoyable.
- Schedule your activities in your journal. Take a moment to schedule your chosen activities in your *My Best Me Journal*, using the "Year at a Glance" section to block out time for your favorite gatherings, reflection moments, or rituals. This will help you stay organized and ensure you carve out space for the things that matter most during Q4.
- Check in with yourself regularly. Schedule time for personal check-ins throughout the quarter. Ask yourself, *Am I staying present and intentional? Am I taking care of myself and finding time to unwind during the busy holiday season?* Adjust your plans to keep the focus on enjoying the season rather than feeling overwhelmed.
- End the year with gratitude. As December winds down, reflect on the highlights of the year, even in the quiet moments. Consider starting a gratitude list, where you jot down one thing each day that brought you joy or peace during Q4.

Notes

Part Five

Yearly

A Year of Intentional Joy

Part 5 is your road map to embracing year-round joy through intentional hobbies and small celebrations. From peaceful indoor moments to outdoor adventures, it's about living with purpose and creating space for what lights you up, while staying offline and in the moment. Ready to make every season feel fresh and inspired? Let's craft a year you'll love, one hobby at a time.

18.

Living with Purpose

What makes you excited to wake up in the morning? Have you ever lost track of time doing something you love? That's the magic of flow, where hobbies and rituals connect you to a deeper sense of purpose. Whether it's a creative pursuit, a mindful ritual, or simply spending time in nature, these small moments shape our fulfillment. In this chapter, we'll explore how embracing activities that bring joy can create a more intentional and meaningful life, using the Japanese concept of ikigai as a guide.

Understanding Hobbies: **The Ikigai Concept**

The Japanese word "ikigai" translates to "a reason for being." It's about living with purpose, waking up each day with something to look forward to, and engaging in activities that bring joy and fulfillment. In Japanese culture, this concept is deeply intertwined with daily habits and hobbies.

Hobbies and Purpose

Hobbies are more than just pastimes; they can be pathways to discovering your ikigai. Painting, gardening, rock climbing, or dancing are all hobbies that offer a chance to engage deeply with your core values and interests. This engagement often leads to a state of flow, where you lose track of time and feel a deep sense of satisfaction.

Finding Hobbies That Spark Joy

Not sure what hobby speaks to you? No worries! Let's find something that aligns with your interests and brings you that sense of purpose. Here's a quick exercise to help you figure out what hobbies might feel like a good fit (for more on hobbies, check out part 4):

- ★ **Reflect on what you enjoy.** Think about the activities that light you up. What do you look forward to doing in your free time? Is it drawing, dancing, or baking? Jot down a few things you already enjoy doing, even if you haven't done them in a while.
- ★ **What makes you lose track of time?** Do you ever get so wrapped up in something that hours fly by without you noticing? That's a sign of flow, a state where you're fully immersed in the activity. Write down any moments when you've felt that way.
- ★ **Try something new.** If you're still unsure, think about things you've always wanted to try. Maybe you've been curious about pottery, or you've always wanted to take up hiking. Write down two to three new activities you'd like to explore.
- ★ **Check in with your values.** Consider what's important to you. Is it creativity, relaxation, adventure, or connection? What hobbies align with those values? For example, if connection is key for you, consider joining a group or community activity.
- ★ **Start small.** Once you've got some ideas, pick one and dedicate a little time to it each week. You don't have to jump all in–just give it a try and see how it feels. Hobbies grow when you nurture them, so don't be afraid to experiment and adjust as you go.

Forest Bathing (Shinrin-Yoku)

In Japan, the practice of shinrin-yoku, or forest bathing, is common and widely encouraged. This involves spending time in nature, which helps you feel more attuned and linked to the natural world. It's a way to disconnect from digital distractions and reconnect with the simplicity and beauty of the natural environment.

Living an Unhurried Life

Ikigai encourages living an unhurried life, always saying to oneself "Slow down" and "Relax." In *Ikigai: The Japanese Secret to a Long and Happy Life,* authors Héctor García and Francesc Miralles recommend going to bed early, waking up early, and enjoying peaceful activities like walking and spending time with friends. Enjoying the little things and each season as it comes is a core part of this philosophy.

Rituals over Goals

Instead of focusing solely on achieving goals, ikigai emphasizes the importance of daily rituals. These rituals, ranging from a morning tea to an evening walk, help create a rhythm in life that is both fulfilling and sustainable. Rituals allow for moments of microflow, turning routine tasks into something enjoyable and meaningful.

Moments of Microflow

Engaging in hobbies and daily rituals can create moments of microflow, when you become fully absorbed in what you're doing. This could be something as simple as washing dishes, where the process itself becomes a source of relaxation and clarity.

Practical Steps to Integrate Ikigai into Your Life

★ **Identify your hobbies.**
Make a list of activities you enjoy and feel passionate about. Include both current hobbies and activities you've been curious to try.

★ **Schedule regular time for hobbies.**
Set aside dedicated times each week for your hobbies. Treat these times as nonnegotiable appointments with yourself.

★ **Engage in nature.**
Practice forest bathing by spending time in nature, whether during a walk in the park or a hike in the woods. Use these moments to disconnect from digital devices and reconnect with the natural world.

★ **Create daily rituals.**
Establish simple daily rituals that bring you joy and help you start or end your day positively. Examples: morning tea, evening walks, or bedtime reading sessions.

★ **Embrace slow living.**
Consciously slow down your pace of life. Take time to enjoy meals, conversations, and activities without rushing. Focus on being present in each moment, savoring the experience fully.

By embracing these principles of ikigai in your daily routine, you'll start to notice a shift—a little less screen time and a lot more presence. You'll feel more connected to what truly matters, and that sense of purpose will spill over into everything you do. It's about finding those small but powerful moments that remind you life's not just about getting through the day; it's about savoring each step along the way.

Key Takeaways

UNDERSTANDING IKIGAI AND HOBBIES: Ikigai is the Japanese concept of finding purpose and joy in daily life. Hobbies are more than just pastimes—they create flow and fulfillment, connecting you to your core values.

FINDING HOBBIES THAT SPARK JOY: Reflect on activities you enjoy, moments when time flies, or hobbies you've always wanted to try. Align your hobbies with your values, such as creativity, relaxation, or connection.

FOREST BATHING (SHINRIN-YOKU): Spend intentional time in nature to reconnect and recharge. Forest bathing reduces stress and fosters a sense of calm and balance.

LIVING AN UNHURRIED LIFE: Embrace slow living by enjoying small moments and seasonal changes. Focus on peaceful rituals over goal-chasing to cultivate sustainable fulfillment.

CREATING MOMENTS OF MICROFLOW: Daily rituals and hobbies create microflow, bringing mindfulness and relaxation to even routine tasks.

INTEGRATING IKIGAI WITH PRACTICAL STEPS: Identify hobbies, schedule regular time for them, engage in nature, and create joyful rituals. Slow down and savor everyday experiences, from meals to conversations.

Action Items

- Make a list of hobbies you enjoy or are curious to try.
- Block out a few times this week for hobbies and treat them as nonnegotiable appointments.
- Choose at least one day this week to spend a minimum of 30 minutes in nature—e.g., walking in a park or exploring a nearby trail.
- Add a simple daily ritual like morning tea or an evening walk to your routine for moments of calm.
- Consciously slow down daily activities, like taking mindful breaks and enjoying meals without rushing.
- Identify routine tasks (e.g., cooking, cleaning) and approach them mindfully to find clarity and relaxation.
- Choose one new hobby from your list to explore this month and dedicate as many days a week to it as you can.

Notes

19.

Life Time Buckets

We often think we have endless time to do the things that matter most—until suddenly life gets in the way. Life Time Buckets offer a way to be intentional about experiences, goals, and priorities at different stages of life, ensuring we don't postpone joy or meaningful pursuits. Instead of waiting for the "perfect time," this chapter helps you map out what you want to do and when, so you can make the most of each season of life. Whether it's adventure in your 20s, deepening relationships in your 30s, or legacy-building in later years, Life Time Buckets act as a guide to aligning your time, energy, and resources with what truly matters.

What Are Life Time Buckets?

The concept of "Life Time Buckets" originates from Bill Perkins's book *Die with Zero*. It is a practical tool for planning life experiences to maximize enjoyment and fulfillment throughout the different stages of life. The idea is to visualize your life as a series of buckets, each representing different decades, such as your 20s, 30s, 40s, and so on. Each bucket is then allocated specific experiences and goals that are most appropriate for that period.

Why Life Time Buckets Are Helpful

Life Time Buckets are like your personal guide to making sure you're spending your time, energy, and money on the experiences that make the most sense for where you are in life. Think of it this way: When you're younger and full of energy, it's the perfect time for physically demanding activities like snowboarding or backpacking. But as you get older, it's totally natural to swap out those activities for something a little less intense—like learning a new skill or diving into a hobby that lights you up. So match your focus to what feels right for you, no matter what stage of life you're in.

A Balanced Perspective

There's no right or wrong way to live your life. This philosophy isn't about setting strict rules or timelines but rather recognizing that life stages come with natural shifts in energy and focus. While some activities may feel more suited to certain phases in life, slowing down or shifting gears can bring its own kind of joy and growth. Ultimately, the concept of "Life Time Buckets" is just one way to reflect on how you spend your time. It's an interesting tool, but the path you choose is entirely up to you.

Examples of Life Time Buckets

20s to 30s

★ **Travel and adventure:** Engage in physically demanding travel and adventure activities.

★ **Career building:** Focus on career advancement and skill acquisition.

30s to 40s

★ **Family and relationships:** Spend quality time with family and strengthen relationships.

★ **Financial intentionality:** Consider long-term financial goals that align with your personal values.

40s to 50s

★ **Personal development:** Engage in hobbies and activities that promote personal growth.

★ **Health and wellness:** Invest more in health and wellness routines.

50s and beyond

★ **Leisure and relaxation:** Focus on leisure activities and relaxation.

★ **Legacy building:** Think about how you want to make a lasting impact. Would you like to mentor, volunteer, or pass your skills on to someone else? This is the time to reflect and share what you've learned.

This method is helpful for tracking how you spend your time and ensuring that you allocate enough time for activities that matter most to you during a certain age bracket. Example: You might want to travel to Europe for a year. Chances are, doing this at an earlier age is better, because demands on your time later in life—especially if you plan to start a family—can become harder to manage with all those "adult responsibilities."

Your Time, Your Life: A Reflection

To help you start thinking about your own Life Time Buckets, reflect on the following questions:

- ★ What are some experiences you want to have in your 20s, 30s, 40s, etc.?
- ★ Are there any activities you've been postponing that might be more enjoyable now than later?
- ★ How can you start reallocating your time and resources to ensure you make the most of each life stage?

Step 1: Reflect on Personal Values

Before diving into your goals, let's start with what truly lights you up. Your Life Time Buckets should reflect what really matters to you, so grab a notebook and think about your core values. What brings you joy? What do you want more of in your life? Is it adventure, family time, creativity, or learning? Set the stage now for everything that follows.

Journal Workout

Take 5 minutes to list your top three personal values. How are they showing up in your life right now? Are there areas where you'd like to make more room for them?

Step 2: Identify Goals and Experiences for Each Life Stage

Now that you have your values front and center, let's dream big! What are the experiences and goals you want to hit at different stages of your life? Think of your 20s, 30s, 40s, and beyond—what do you want to accomplish in those decades? Maybe it's traveling to new places, starting a business, or learning a new hobby. Whatever it is, this is your chance to lay it all out.

Journal Workout

Take 10 minutes to write down three experiences or goals you want to achieve before each big milestone—age 30, 40, 50, etc. Are there any things you've been putting off that you can jump into now?

Step 3: Allocate Resources Toward Your Goals

Now that you've mapped out your goals, it's time to make sure your time, energy, and money are working for you. No need for a total life overhaul—but think about how you can carve out space for what matters. Maybe it's saving a little each month for that big adventure or setting aside regular time to pursue a passion project.

Action item: Life Time Bucket integration. Rather than waiting for the "right time" to take on your goals, work them into your schedule in intentional ways. Here's how you can get started:

★ **Start small with intentional days.** Each morning, choose one small step that aligns with a Life Time Bucket goal. Whether it's reading a chapter of a book, setting aside 10 minutes for language practice, or taking a short walk outside, these micro actions add up.

★ **Incorporate your goal into your current habits.** Pair your Life Time Bucket goal with something you already do often. If your goal is to prioritize wellness, stretch for 5 minutes after brushing your teeth. If creativity is your focus, sketch for a few minutes while your coffee brews.

★ **Set micro milestones.** Instead of thinking in long-term chunks, break your goals into smaller wins. If your bigger goal is to save for a trip, commit to skipping some coffee runs and transferring that money to savings instead. If you want to build a reading habit, aim for just 5 minutes of reading at a time rather than tackling an entire book at once.

★ **Track progress daily, weekly, and monthly.** Before bed each night, do a quick check-in. Did you take one small action toward a meaningful goal today? Use a simple checklist, a reflection in your *My Best Me Journal,* or a sticky note to celebrate small wins. Repeat this habit weekly and monthly, then review your end-of-year achievements—every small win should be celebrated.

The *My Best Me Journal*

Throughout this book, you may notice ideas from the *My Best Me Journal* sprinkled into different activities and reflections. Think of it as your sidekick for living intentionally—a journal meets planner designed by Offline Humans to help you create routines that stick, celebrate those small wins, and take steps that actually feel doable. It's about focusing on what works for you and making each day just a bit more meaningful.

To give you a taste, we've included a few sample pages throughout. You don't need the *My Best Me Journal* to jump in—any notebook will do—but if you're curious to try it out, it's available on OfflineHumans.com. However you choose to join in, these activities are here to make the journey toward a grounded, intentional life feel like something you want to do, not just something you should do.

Why Prioritizing Now Matters

There's no "perfect time" to start working on your Life Time Buckets—life's always going to be busy in one way or another. The key is to start planning now, so you're not waiting for things to magically slow down. Whether you're in your 20s, 30s, or beyond, the earlier you get intentional about your goals, the more freedom you'll have to adapt when life shifts—because it always does.

Example: If you've always wanted to take a sabbatical or travel for a year, it doesn't have to happen in your 20s. You can make it work in your 40s or 50s, too—it just takes a bit more planning. Prioritize now, whenever "now" is for you, and start working toward those dream experiences so they don't get lost in the shuffle.

Little Hacks for Making Time Count

To keep your Life Time Buckets in focus and make sure you're moving steadily toward your goals, try these simple but effective hacks.

Spend 10 minutes each month reviewing your priorities.

A monthly check-in is more realistic, especially if you're like me and love to do this during your Sunday reset planning days. When I look at my week at a glance, I take a moment to reflect on my priorities and make sure I'm aligning my time with what matters most. It's a great way to stay intentional without feeling like you're constantly reassessing.

Keep a weekly journal to track what brings you joy.

This one's simple but powerful. Spend 5 minutes each week jotting down where your energy went and what made you happy. I like to use the *My Best Me Journal* for this—setting up my best-me routine with my nonnegotiables that fill my cup during my morning and night routines. Plus, reflecting on daily celebrations really helps keep the joy front and center.

Schedule Life Time Bucket reflections.

Just like you schedule workouts or meetings, block out time to check in with yourself, monthly, quarterly, or whenever works best for you. This is your chance to review your Life Time Buckets and see if any adjustments are needed. Life gets busy, but keeping these reflections in your calendar ensures you're always moving forward.

Key Takeaways

LIFE TIME BUCKETS AND THEIR PURPOSE: Life Time Buckets help you align your goals and experiences with different stages of life.

IMPLEMENTING LIFE TIME BUCKETS: Use your 20s, 30s, 40s, and beyond to focus on what matters most in each phase.

LIFE TIME BUCKETS ASSESSMENT: Reflect on your personal values to guide how you spend your time and energy.

Action Items

- Take 5 minutes to list your top three core values and reflect on how they show up in your life.
- Write down three experiences or goals for each major life stage (e.g., 20s, 30s, 40s, etc.).
- Plan one day a week to work toward a specific Life Time Bucket goal.
- Use a journal or planner to review your goals, reflect on wins, and adjust as needed.
- Block out regular check-ins (monthly, quarterly, and yearly) to revisit your Life Time Buckets and make any necessary changes.

Notes

20.

Year at a Glance

Think of the "Year at a Glance" as your bird's-eye view of the year. It's like pulling out a map before you start a road trip, except this one isn't about highways—it's about milestones, goals, and all the little (and big) things you want to achieve in the next twelve months. The idea is simple: When you can see your whole year laid out, you'll be better equipped to stay on track, make adjustments, and most importantly, celebrate your wins as they come.

Your Road Map for the Year Ahead

Why do a "Year at a Glance"? Well, it's not just for organization, though that's a nice perk. Rather, it's about giving yourself the space to dream big, set intentions, and track your progress as you move through each season. You'll be able to spot patterns, stay focused on what matters, and avoid that dreaded feeling of time slipping away unnoticed. Whether you're marking down personal goals and work milestones or planning for those much-needed pauses, the "Year at a Glance" helps you create a road map for the life you want to live—one step at a time.

And the best part? You'll have a sample page from the *My Best Me Journal* to guide you, with everything you need in one place—habit trackers, goals, and reflection prompts all designed to help you stay grounded and on top of your game throughout the year.

Breaking Down the Year

Now that you have the full year in view, it's time to break it down. Rather than looking at the next twelve months as one big stretch of time (which can feel a little overwhelming), the "Year at a Glance" helps you divide and conquer by splitting the year into quarters. Each quarter is a new chapter; whether you're focusing on personal growth, work milestones, or seasonal rituals, breaking the year into smaller chunks gives you room to breathe.

You can start by assigning a theme or focus to each quarter. For example:

- **Q1 brings in the fresh starts and setting new habits.**
- **Q2 could focus on creative projects or outdoor adventures as the weather warms.**
- **Q3 can be the time to reflect, recharge, or revisit those midyear goals.**
- **Q4 wraps up the year with a focus on winding down, celebrating wins, and looking ahead to the next chapter.**

Each quarter becomes its own mini journey, allowing you to be intentional with your time and energy. And if life throws you a curveball? No problem! Each quarter is a chance to reset and readjust your path.

Year at a Glance

	January		February		March
1	yearly intentions journal sesh	1		1	
2	start 30-day offline challenge	2		2	
3		3	Attend Bible study	3	
4	finalize Q1 project proposal	4		4	
5	budget review for January	5	10K local fun run	5	Attend wellness retreat
6	Lisa's b-day	6		6	
7		7		7	
8	First day at work	8		8	My birthday, yay!
9		9	Project due	9	
10		10		10	
11		11		11	
12		12		12	Start 6-wk strength training
13	Bookstore brunch with Jenn	13		13	
14		14	Valentine's Day	14	
15	Half marathon registration	15		15	
16		16	Family visits	16	
17		17		17	
18		18		18	
19		19		19	Review progress, adjust goals
20	WEEKEND GETAWAY	20	Office closed, President's Day	20	Start of spring
21	WEEKEND GETAWAY	21		21	
22	Meal prep Sundays begin	22		22	
23		23		23	
24		24		24	
25		25		25	
26	Finalize YT scripts	26	Plan springtime hiking trip	26	Plan vegetable garden
27		27		27	
28		28	Quarterly report due	28	Solo day trip
29		29		29	
30	Finance recap	30		30	Q1 recap/evaluation
31		31		31	Team-building activity

January goals

- ✓ read at least one book
- ✓ learn two new skills
- ✓ keep up with self-care routine

February goals

- ✓ build strong friendships
- ✓ start daily journal tracking
- ✓ learn new healthy recipes

March goals

- ✓ join a new group to meet people
- ✓ plan trip to a new place
- ✓ establish a healthy routine

Inspiration Guide

Sometimes, the hardest part of starting something new is knowing where to begin. That's why the *My Best Me Journal* includes prompts and templates to guide you through the process of filling out your "Year at a Glance." But don't worry—this isn't about perfection. It's about starting somewhere and letting your entries evolve throughout the year.

For example, here's how I might fill out the first quarter of the year:

- ★ Q1 theme: Focus on daily rituals and building momentum.
- ★ January: Start with morning routines, moving my body, and creating space for reflection.
- ★ February: Focus on personal projects, but keep up with those foundational habits.
- ★ March: Prepare for a spring reset—reflect on what's worked so far and tweak habits as needed.

Reflection and Adaptability

The beauty of the "Year at a Glance" isn't that you lock yourself into rigid goals or plans. Life happens, and that's okay. The magic of this process is its flexibility. As you go through the year, you'll have moments when things go exactly as planned—and other times when they don't.

That's why it's important to treat your "Year at a Glance" as a living document. Think of it as your guide, not your rulebook. Every few months, take a moment to reflect on how things are going. What's working? What isn't? Maybe a goal you set in January no longer aligns with where you are by May, or perhaps life threw a few unexpected challenges at you. That's where the power of reflection comes in.

By regularly revisiting and adjusting your plan, you can keep moving forward with intention, without feeling like you've failed if things don't go perfectly. The *My Best Me Journal* is designed to grow with you, helping you navigate life's twists and turns while staying true to what matters most.

At its core, the "Year at a Glance" isn't solely about goal setting—it's about creating space for intentional pauses throughout the year, be it a monthly self-care day, a weekend to disconnect, or a seasonal reset. Planning these moments into your year ensures you're not just grinding from one month to the next without coming up for air.

This approach aligns perfectly with the Offline Humans philosophy—living mindfully and embracing the rituals that keep us grounded. You can use the "Year at a Glance" to schedule these pauses, marking down time for rituals like journaling, meditation, or spending a day completely offline.

By tying these intentional rituals into your year, you create a flow that balances productivity with rest, achievement with reflection. This balance helps you move through the year with a sense of purpose, without feeling burned out.

Your ______ Year at a Glance

Now it's time to make your year your own! With your "Year at a Glance" laid out, you have the perfect tool to start planning, dreaming, and reflecting on what's ahead. Use this sample page from the *My Best Me Journal* as a guide, and feel free to tweak it to fit your personal style.

January	February	March
January goals	**February goals**	**March goals**
• ______	• ______	• ______
• ______	• ______	• ______
• ______	• ______	• ______

April	May	June

April goals

-
-
-

May goals

-
-
-

June goals

-
-
-

July		August		September	

July goals

-
-
-

August goals

-
-
-

September goals

-
-
-

October		November		December	

October goals

-
-
-

November goals

-
-
-

December goals

-
-
-

Want more inspiration? The *My Best Me Journal* is your go-to tool for mindful growth, with habit trackers, reflection prompts, and space to set your intentions. You can grab yours at OfflineHumans.com, and follow us on Instagram @OfflineHumans for more tips, rituals, and behind-the-scenes inspiration for living your best offline life.

21.

Reflections in Progress

A Year of Journal Workout Prompts

In this chapter, it's time to pause, reflect, and reconnect with your journey—one prompt at a time. Think of journaling as hitting the pause button on life for a moment. It's not merely about jotting down your thoughts but about giving yourself a little time out to reconnect and check in with the inner voice we sometimes overlook. Each of these prompts in this chapter is a gentle nudge, guiding you toward those thoughts that might otherwise stay buried in the busyness of everyday life.

You don't have to journal daily to make an impact. Maybe it's once a week during a quiet Sunday morning, or a few minutes each evening to unwind. Find what rhythm works for you—there's no right or wrong way to fit this in. The goal isn't to become a writer; it's simply to build a habit of self-reflection that keeps you grounded and connected to what lights you up.

In this chapter, you'll find prompts centered around creating rituals, finding your place in your community, and setting intentions. Each theme is its own little journey, with questions designed to help you get real with yourself. No pressure, no rigid schedule—just a few moments to be with your thoughts.

Curious? Let's explore the first theme: rituals.

Rituals

Rituals aren't just routines—they're the intentional moments that ground us, give us meaning, and help us slow down in a fast-paced world. Be it your morning cup of tea, a walk in the park, or an evening journaling session, rituals offer us pockets of peace and purpose and help us reconnect with ourselves by creating moments of mindfulness throughout the day. This prompt theme encourages you to discover and cultivate those rituals in your life. Think about the moments that bring you comfort, joy, or a sense of calm. How can you turn them into meaningful rituals that enrich your daily life?

1. What small activities already bring you a sense of calm or joy? Think of those little things you do regularly—reading before bed, stretching in the morning, or savoring a quiet cup of coffee. How can you be more intentional about turning them into daily or weekly rituals?

2. What new rituals can you introduce into your life? Is there something you've been wanting to try but haven't made time for? Maybe it's a mindful morning routine, daily journaling, or a weekly offline break. Now's the time to explore how you can fit these into your life.

3. How do your rituals help you reconnect with yourself? Reflect on how your current rituals make you feel. Do they help you disconnect from the chaos? Do they bring you clarity or calm? If not, what changes could you make to ensure your rituals support your well-being?

Remember, rituals don't have to be complicated or time-consuming. Find what works for you and create intentional pauses that give you space to breathe.

Community

Community is more than the people around you—it's the sense of belonging, support, and purpose that comes from being part of something bigger than yourself. In Japanese culture, the concept of ikigai—finding your reason for being—often involves community and how we connect with others to find meaning. From family and friends to a broader group, community plays a vital role in shaping who we are and how we experience life. This prompt is about reflecting on your connection to community and how it supports your well-being.

1. What communities do you currently feel most connected to? These could be close-knit circles like family and friends or broader groups like work, social cliques, or online communities. How do these connections add value to your life?

2. How does being part of a community contribute to your sense of purpose? Think about the ways in which your community supports you, motivates you, or challenges you to grow. How do these connections help you find meaning in your everyday life?

3. What steps can you take to strengthen your sense of community? Are there relationships you'd like to nurture more? Or are there perhaps new communities you want to explore or contribute to? Reflect on how you can invest in these connections.

Community is about support, sharing experiences, and finding your place within the larger picture. It's one of the pillars that help us thrive, and nurturing it brings a deeper sense of purpose to our lives.

Intention

Setting intentions is like charting your course, consciously deciding how you want to show up in your life, rather than drifting through it on autopilot. Intentions are more flexible than goals; they're not only about what you want to achieve but also about how you want to feel and who you want to become in the process. This prompt will help you explore your intentions and how they align with your deeper values.

1. What intentions are you setting for yourself right now? Think about your current focus–personal growth, work, relationships, etc. How do you want to approach these areas of your life? What's the guiding intention behind them?

2. How do your intentions align with your values? Reflect on what truly matters to you–balance, creativity, connection, or something else entirely. Are your intentions in harmony with your core values, or do they need a little realignment?

3. What small steps can you take to live more intentionally each day? It doesn't have to be big. Small, mindful actions–like starting your day with gratitude, taking a moment to pause before reacting, or being more present with loved ones–can shift how you experience your life.

Remember, intentions are fluid. They are the direction you're headed, not rigid goals you have to meet. Revisit and refine them as you grow.

Protection Time Circle

In a world where time feels like a limited resource, creating boundaries around how you spend your time is an essential form of self-care. This is what we call your "Protection Time Circle," a space where you guard your most valuable moments from distractions, overwhelm, and external demands. It's about carving out time for yourself and your priorities, so you can stay focused on what truly matters. This prompt encourages you to reflect on how you protect your time and what changes you can make to ensure your time is spent intentionally.

1. What activities or commitments tend to take away from your personal time? Identify the distractions or unnecessary obligations that often steal your focus and energy. How can you limit or eliminate those to protect your time circle?

2. How can you create stronger boundaries around your time? Reflect on areas where you need clearer boundaries–whether it's with work, social media, or personal relationships. How can you say no, to protect your time for what's most important?

3. What are your nonnegotiables when it comes to your time? Think about the activities or rituals you absolutely don't want to compromise on, like your morning routine, family time, or creative projects. How can you ensure these priorities stay protected within your time circle?

Remember, your time is precious, and how you protect it reflects how you care for yourself and your well-being. Guarding your time circle helps you stay grounded and intentional in a busy world.

Connecting to Online Time

In the digital age, it's easy to lose track of time spent online. From endless scrolling to checking notifications, our online habits often disconnect us from the present moment. This prompt is about reflecting on your relationship with the time you spend online and finding ways to use it more intentionally. The goal with this prompt isn't to cut out your online time entirely but rather to create a healthy balance and be mindful of how your time online impacts your day-to-day life.

1. How do you feel after spending a significant amount of time online? Do you feel drained, anxious, or disconnected? Does certain online content bring you joy and inspiration? Reflect on how your online habits affect your mood and energy levels.

2. Which online activities add value to your life, and which ones feel like distractions? Identify the types of online content or platforms that enrich your life, and those that tend to waste your time. How can you adjust your online habits to focus more on the valuable content?

3. What changes can you make to be more intentional with your online time? Maybe it's setting time limits for social media, scheduling offline hours during your day, or creating a list of productive online activities. How can you connect more consciously with the time you spend online?

The aim here is to take back control of your time online, making it a tool that enhances your life rather than detracting from it.

Time Buckets for Your Life

Imagine your time as a collection of buckets (not to be confused with the concept of "Life Time Buckets," covered in chapter 19!), each one holding a different part of your life–work, relationships, self-care, and everything in between. Now here's the fun part: Some buckets might be overflowing, splashing water everywhere (I'm looking at you, work), while others are sitting there barely filled. This prompt is about balancing those buckets so one isn't tipping over while the others run dry.

1. What are the main time buckets in your life? Picture the buckets of your life–what are their labels? Work, family, hobbies, friends? Grab a pen, and write down what your main buckets are. Do they feel balanced?

2. Which buckets are leaking, and which ones are practically overflowing? Are you accidentally filling one bucket (like work) to the brim while others (like self-care or fun) are practically empty? How can you patch up the leaks and spread the water a little more evenly?

3. What's one small shift you can make to balance your buckets? Maybe your self-care bucket is looking a little dry. How can you pour more into it–whether it's blocking out time for a morning walk or sitting down with a cup of tea? What's a simple way to keep all your buckets steady and full?

By keeping your time buckets in check, you can make sure you're not drowning in one area while another part of your life gets left high and dry.

Unfollow Spree

Your social-media feed should feel like a place of inspiration, not an overwhelming tidal wave of content you don't even care about. It's time for a digital declutter—a satisfying unfollow spree. Think of this as the social-media version of clearing out your closet: Toss anything that no longer fits, sparks joy, or serves you.

1. Who's on the unfollow list? Scroll through your feed with a fresh perspective. If someone's posts make you feel stressed, annoyed, or just meh, it's time to hit that unfollow button and clean out the digital clutter to make space for the accounts that lift you up.

2. Create your "inspo-only" feed. Now, instead of only unfollowing, replace that space with something better. Curate a feed that fills you with inspiration, creativity, and good vibes. Whom do you actually want to see when you scroll through your feed? This is your chance to build a space that motivates and uplifts you.

3. Set a regular declutter routine. Don't let the clutter creep back in! Mark your calendar for a quick quarterly unfollow spree, so your feed stays fresh and aligned with your current vibe.

By decluttering your digital life, you create space for more intentional online interactions—and, yes, this one feels just as satisfying as cleaning out your closet.

Joy Writing

Let's talk about joy—the little sparks that make your day brighter and your heart lighter. Joy can be found in the smallest of moments, and it's something worth celebrating, documenting, and chasing. This prompt is all about identifying the things that bring you genuine happiness and making sure there's room for them in your life.

1. What's lighting you up right now? Think about the moments in your day that make you smile—that first sip of coffee, an afternoon walk, or a funny text from a friend. Write down the things that instantly boost your mood.

2. What brings you joy that you've been neglecting? Is there something that used to make you happy but that you haven't made time for lately? Maybe it's dancing, reading, or crafting. Reflect on what's been missing from your life, and make a plan to bring it back.

3. How can you sprinkle more joy into your everyday routine? Joy doesn't have to be saved for special occasions. What small things can you do to bring more joy into your daily life? Perhaps it's setting aside 10 minutes for yourself each morning or planning a weekend adventure. The goal is to infuse your days with moments that make you feel truly alive.

By focusing on what brings you joy, you create a life that feels more vibrant and fulfilling—one joyful moment at a time.

Barriers

We all have them—those invisible (and sometimes not-so-invisible) barriers that keep us from living the way we want to. It could be time, self-doubt, or the overwhelming busyness of life. This prompt is about identifying those barriers and figuring out how to knock them down—or at least climb over them.

1. What's currently standing in your way? Is it time, energy, motivation, or something else? Be honest with yourself—what's the one thing that's been blocking your path lately? Identifying the barriers is the first step toward breaking them down.

2. What's one small change that could help you overcome these barriers? You don't have to move mountains all at once. What's a small step you can take to start clearing the path? Maybe it's setting a boundary, asking for help, or simply giving yourself permission to slow down.

3. How can you reframe these barriers as opportunities? Sometimes the things that seem like obstacles are actually opportunities for growth. What's one barrier you can flip on its head? How can you use it as a chance to learn something new or change your approach?

Remember, barriers are just bumps in the road. With a little reflection and some creative thinking, you can find ways to work around them and keep moving forward.

Quarterly Check-Ins

Each quarter is like a new chapter in your year—a time to reflect, adjust, and realign with your goals and intentions. Quarterly check-ins are your chance to pause, look back at what's working, and reset where needed. Whether you're celebrating wins or pivoting toward something new, these prompts will help you stay grounded, intentional, and focused on what matters most.

January–March: What's your momentum?

The start of the year often brings a burst of fresh energy, but let's be honest—sometimes that motivation fizzles out before spring even arrives. This is your chance to reflect on the goals you've set and the progress you've made. Are you building momentum, or are some of your goals still stuck in the to-do pile?

★ **What's one specific win from Q1 that you're proud of?** Think big or small—maybe you stuck with a new habit or tackled a personal project.

★ **What's been the biggest challenge so far?** Reflect on any roadblocks, and consider how you can move past them.

★ **Looking ahead to Q2, what's one goal you want to pursue with more focus?** Now's the time to refine, adjust, or double down on what matters most.

April–June: What's blooming?

Spring is about growth, both literally and metaphorically. As nature begins to wake up, what's starting to bloom in your life? Use this quarter to reflect on the seeds you've planted—a new habit, a work goal, a creative project—and how you can continue to nurture them.

★ **What new ideas, habits, or opportunities have popped up for you this quarter?** Think about how you can nurture them moving forward.

★ **Is there anything that hasn't taken root yet?** It's okay if something hasn't worked out—now's the time to adjust or let go of what's not serving you.

★ **Looking ahead to summer, what's one goal or intention you want to nurture as the days get longer?** Think of this as planting seeds for the next season.

July–September: Are you still aligned?

Summer's heat might slow things down, but it's also a great time to reflect on whether your goals and intentions are still aligned with where you want to be. As you approach the second half of the year, check in with how you're feeling. Are you on track, or is it time for a course correction?

- ★ **What's one thing you've learned about yourself in the first half of the year?** Consider how you can use that insight to fuel the second half of the year.
- ★ **Are there any goals or intentions you've drifted away from?** Reflect on whether it's time to recommit to them or adjust your focus.
- ★ **What's one thing you can do this quarter to realign your goals with your values?** Maybe it's taking a step back or pushing ahead with more focus.

October–December: What are you celebrating?

As the year comes to a close, it's time to reflect on all you've accomplished–big or small–and celebrate your journey. Whether you've crushed your goals or taken small, steady steps toward them, this is your chance to acknowledge how far you've come.

- ★ **What's one major accomplishment from the year that deserves celebrating?** Don't be afraid to pat yourself on the back for a job well done!
- ★ **What's a smaller win that maybe went unnoticed but deserves recognition?** Sometimes the little things–like sticking to a habit or learning something new–are just as important.
- ★ **What's one thing you're excited about for the next year?** Reflect on how you've grown and how that growth will carry you into the year ahead.

Extra Journaling Space

Celebrations

Celebrations aren't just for big milestones—they're for all the little victories that make up the journey. Whether it's a major goal you've crushed or a small, quiet win that helped you grow, taking the time to acknowledge and celebrate is key to staying motivated and connected to your progress. This section is about looking back, recognizing your achievements, and giving yourself the space to celebrate, reflect, and feel proud of the steps you've taken throughout the year.

Celebrating Personal Growth

Sometimes growth is subtle, and other times it's life-changing. Either way, it's important to pause and celebrate how you've evolved, whether that's emotionally, mentally, or spiritually.

★ **What's one way you've grown this year that you're proud of?** Perhaps you've become more patient, embraced a new mindset, or learned to let go of something that no longer serves you.

★ **How did this growth impact your day-to-day life?** Reflect on how these changes have shaped who you are and how you interact with the world.

★ **What's one thing you can do to celebrate this personal growth?** Treat yourself to a quiet evening, journal about the experience, or share it with a loved one—one way or another, find a way to honor this progress.

Celebrating Your Journey

The journey is often just as important as the destination. This prompt encourages you to celebrate not just the outcomes but also the process—the ups, the downs, and everything in between.

- ★ **What's one challenge you overcame this year, and how did it shape your journey?** Reflect on a tough moment or obstacle that helped you grow stronger or more resilient.
- ★ **How did your journey evolve throughout the year?** Think about how your intentions and goals shifted over time, and celebrate the flexibility and adaptability you've shown.
- ★ **What's one ritual or tradition you can create to celebrate your journey moving forward?** Whether it's with an end-of-year reflection, a personal celebration, or a quiet moment of gratitude, make space to honor the journey as it continues.

Celebrations are about more than just the big wins—they're about recognizing your growth, honoring your progress, and finding joy in the process. By taking time to reflect and celebrate, you keep yourself motivated and connected to the intentional life you're building.

Challenge—1,000 Hours Unplugged

Screens have a way of taking over our lives. From social media to video streaming to the never-ending emails, it's easy to lose hours online without realizing it. The 1,000 Hours Unplugged challenge is here to help you reclaim that time—one hour at a time. The goal is simple but powerful: Spend 1,000 hours unplugged over the course of a year. That's roughly 2.75 hours a day spent away from screens, dedicated to real-life experiences, creativity, and connection. Think you're up for it? Let's break it down and get started!

What's my favorite way to unplug? Is it taking a walk, reading a book, or spending time with friends? Think about what activities make you feel the most connected to yourself when you're not glued to a screen. List a few go-to unplugged activities that you can turn to whenever you need a break.

How can I make unplugging a daily habit? Brainstorm small, practical ways to integrate more unplugged time into your routine. Maybe it's starting your morning screen-free, designating offline hours during dinner, or taking a tech-free evening walk. What's one small change you can commit to today?

Track my unplugged time. Use the *My Best Me Journal* or another tracker to log your unplugged hours each week. Seeing your progress will motivate you to keep going—and remind you of all the meaningful moments that happen when you're not looking at a screen. How close can you get to that 1,000-hour goal by the end of the year?

Bonus Journal Workout: Screen-Time Check-Ins. Every so often, check in on your screen-time stats. Are you spending more time online than you realized? Use these check-ins as a way to reset and adjust—turning more of your time into unplugged moments that fuel your creativity, relationships, and well-being.

The 1,000 Hours Unplugged challenge isn't about perfection; it's about making intentional choices to spend more time in the real world and less time lost in the digital one. One hour at a time, you're creating more space for the things that matter.

Challenge—Best Me Reset

Sometimes life gets busy, and it's easy to lose track of your routines, goals, and personal well-being. The Best Me Reset challenge is designed to help you hit the reset button and realign with the habits and intentions that make you feel your best. This challenge isn't about a complete overhaul—it's about small daily actions that bring you back to your center, helping you refocus, recharge, and step into each day with more intention. Feel free to switch things up! The twelve habits in this challenge are interchangeable between morning and evening, so you can customize the routine to fit your day. Whether you prefer reflecting in the morning or moving your body in the evening, the goal is to build a rhythm that works for you.

Morning Reset

- ★ **Wake up before 8 a.m.** Early mornings offer a fresh start. Set your alarm for before 8 a.m. to give yourself time to ease into the day with focus and intention.
- ★ **Put yourself before your phone.** Resist the urge to check your phone first thing in the morning. Take some time for yourself—a quiet moment with a cup of tea, stretching, or journaling—before diving into the digital world.
- ★ **Move your body.** Aim for at least 30 minutes of movement each day. A brisk walk, yoga, or a workout can boost your energy and set a positive tone for the day.
- ★ **Stay off social media before 9 a.m.** Start your day with clarity and focus by keeping your morning screen-free. By pushing back your social-media time, you allow yourself to prioritize real-life connections and productivity.
- ★ **Track your habits.** Use the *My Best Me Journal* to log your daily habits, goals, and reflections. This keeps you accountable and helps you track your progress throughout the challenge.
- ★ **Incorporate feel-good rituals.** Build feel-good moments into your morning routine—for example, getting dressed in something that makes you feel confident, doing mirror affirmations, or enjoying a mindful breakfast. These little rituals help set a positive tone for the day.

Evening Reset

- ★ **Do something fun daily.** Life is about balance! Each day, make time to do something that brings you joy, whether it's a creative hobby, spending time with loved ones, or unwinding with a good book.
- ★ **Walk for 15 minutes, completely offline.** Take a 15-minute walk without your phone in nature or around your neighborhood to help you clear your mind and reconnect with the world around you.
- ★ **Plan your day.** Before bed, jot down a few key tasks or intentions for the next day. This simple habit helps you wake up feeling organized and ready to tackle your priorities.
- ★ **Reflect and celebrate.** Take a moment to reflect on your day. What went well? What are you proud of? Celebrate the small wins and make note of anything you want to improve tomorrow.
- ★ **Do your evening wind-down ritual.** Create a bedtime routine that helps you unwind, like dimming the lights, reading a book, or practicing gratitude. This prepares your mind and body for rest.
- ★ **Have a moment of quiet realignment.** Take a few minutes for quiet reflection, prayer, or journaling. This is your time to realign with your goals and intentions, offering space to connect with your inner self before the day ends.

The Best Me Reset challenge is about making small, mindful changes that lead to big results. With the support of your *My Best Me Journal*, you'll have everything you need in one place to track your habits, reflect on your progress, and continue growing into the best version of yourself.

Ready to reset and step into a more intentional version of you? Join the community! You're not alone on this journey—connect with others who are also taking on the Best Me Reset challenge by following our Instagram account @OfflineHumans. Share your progress, find inspiration, and be part of a supportive community that's committed to intentional living and mindful growth. Let's reset together!

Conclusion

Join the Movement: Offline, Together

Ready to take your journey to the next level? Here's where the real fun begins—by becoming part of a community of like-minded people all striving to unplug, recharge, and live their best lives offline. You're not merely joining a challenge—you're joining a movement.

To make it even easier (and a little more fun!), we've put together free resources like downloadable habit trackers, challenge prompts, and tips to help you stay on track throughout the year. Plus, you'll get access to our exclusive community on Instagram, where we share progress, inspiration, and a few surprises along the way.

Head over to our Instagram account @OfflineHumans, and join the conversation. Use the hashtag #BestMeChallenge to track your progress and connect with others who are taking part. Every week, we spotlight challenge participants, share stories, and offer support to help you through it. It's a blast seeing how we all evolve together!

The Offline Mark:
A Visual Commitment to Living Offline

Let's make it official! Imagine a simple, symbolic gesture to remind ourselves to live offline. We're calling it the "Offline Mark." Try writing the word "OFFLINE" on your palm or wrist as a reminder to be fully present.

If it feels right to you, snap a quick picture, share it on socials, then log off. Research shows that doing things alongside others, even virtually, can boost commitment and make habits stick. This small gesture shows the world (and yourself) that you're taking time to disconnect. Whether you're stepping away for a weekend reset or building new habits, you're part of a quiet reminder that sometimes the best moments happen without a screen in sight.

Final Action Items

Everything we've explored together in this book is about creating space for mindful, intentional living. It's not about doing everything perfectly but rather embracing the small changes that bring you closer to the life you want to live.

Whenever you feel stuck or overwhelmed, remember that this book is always here to guide you. Whether it's a daily, weekly, or monthly check-in, you can open these pages anytime you need a little inspiration to reset, refocus, and go offline. Use it as a tool to stay grounded, reconnect with yourself, and live more intentionally.

* **Continue reflecting.** Make time for regular check-ins with yourself. Use the quarterly prompts and your *My Best Me Journal*, or simply set aside a few minutes each day to reconnect with your goals and intentions.
* **Embrace flexibility.** Life doesn't always go as planned, and that's okay. Stay flexible, adjust when needed, and allow yourself the grace to shift your focus as life evolves.
* **Join the community.** Connect with others on the same path to intentional living by following @OfflineHumans on your favorite social-media platforms. Whether you're looking for daily tips, inspiring content, or support from a like-minded community, you'll find us there, evolving and growing alongside you.

As you move forward, remember that every step—no matter how small—is a step toward the life you're creating. Keep going, stay intentional, and continue growing into the best version of yourself.

Extra Journaling Space

References

Cameron, Julia. *The Artist's Way: A Spiritual Path to Higher Creativity, 30th Anniversary Edition*. 2016, Tarcher.

Clear, James. *Atomic Habits: An Easy & Proven Way to Build Good Habits & Break Bad Ones.* 2018, Avery.

DeYoung, Kevin. *Crazy Busy: A (Mercifully) Short Book about a (Really) Big Problem.* 2013, Crossway Books.

Dunne, Linnea. *Good Mornings: Morning Rituals for Wellness, Peace and Purpose.* 2019, Gaia.

García, Héctor and Miralles, Francesc. *Ikigai: The Japanese Secret to a Long and Happy Life.* 2017, Penguin Life.

Hari, Johann. *Stolen Focus: Why You Can't Pay Attention–and How to Think Deeply Again.* 2022, Crown.

Intelligent Change. *The Five Minute Journal: The Original Gratitude Journal.*

Knapp, Jake and Zeratsky, John. *Make Time: How to Focus on What Matters Every Day.* 2018, Crown Currency.

Newport, Cal. *Digital Minimalism: Choosing a Focused Life in a Noisy World.* 2019, Portfolio.

Offline Humans. *My Best Me Journal: A Daily Journal for Your Mind, Life & Thoughts.* 2024, Offline Humans.

Perkins, Bill. *Die With Zero: Getting All You Can from Your Money and Your Life.* 2020, Mariner Books.

Shlain, Tiffany. *24/6: The Power of Unplugging One Day a Week.* 2019, Gallery Books.

Ter Kuile, Casper. *The Power of Ritual: Turning Everyday Activities into Soulful Practices.* 2020, HarperOne.

Urban, Melissa. *The Book of Boundaries: Set the Limits That Will Set You Free.* 2022, The Dial Press.

Walker, Rob. *The Art of Noticing: 131 Ways to Spark Creativity, Find Inspiration, and Discover Joy in the Everyday.* 2019, Knopf.

Acknowledgments

To my incredible internet community—my Outties. In college, I used to live by the motto "Never quit your daydream," mostly because I hated school (lol) and always dreamed of becoming a YouTuber. Thank you for making this dream a reality and for constantly encouraging me through every phase of my life. Your support means everything to me.

A mis padres, mis lindos. Lindos, mil gracias por el amor que siempre me demostraron. Ustedes hicieron tantos sacrificios por mí, y nunca me lo echaron en cara—al contrario, siempre fueron padres llenos de amor. Siempre me dejaron soñar y siempre creyeron en mí. Gracias por darme el amor incondicional que siempre necesité, por estar orgullosos de mí y por ser mis mejores amigos.

To Dennis, Dennisita, honey, my husband. Thank you for your love, patience, and constant care. Thank you for holding me through all of life's ups and downs and for always reminding me that I'm capable. Love with you has always been so easy.

To Sabina. You are the best teammate I could have asked for. Thank you for always encouraging me, validating my feelings, and being my go-to for all things with life and work. I appreciate you endlessly—you just get me.

To my team at DK and UTA. Thank you for believing in me and for giving me this chance. I hope this book makes an even bigger impact than we all initially imagined. A special thank you to my editor, Alexander Rigby, for making my first book such a seamless and organized process—you truly taught me the ins and outs of the publishing world. Thank you also to Lindsay Dobbs for the lovely book design, Tiffany Taing for her editorial assistance, and Samantha Silverman for creating all the illustrations.

To my dog, Jupiter. Thanks for being cute, derpy, soft, and the sweetest little distraction when my deadlines for this book project felt a bit overwhelming. I hope you live one thousand years (or at least long enough to understand how much I adore you).

Index

P

Q

R

About the Author

Natalie Alzate, better known as Natalie's Outlet, is a content creator, entrepreneur, and advocate for offline living. With over a decade of expertise in the digital space, Natalie has built a thriving online community through creative storytelling, creative hacks, and lifestyle content, amassing an audience of millions.

Now, through Offline Humans, Natalie is leading a movement toward living offline, encouraging people to embrace moments of pause and mindfulness in a hyper-digital world. She has created products like the *My Best Me Journal,* designed to help people track their habits and personal growth, and Ritual Teas, crafted to turn everyday moments into mindful rituals.

With both her content and her products, Natalie continues to inspire others to reconnect with themselves, their goals, and the world around them—one offline moment at a time.